Our Debt to Greece and Rome

EDITORS
GEORGE DEPUE HADZSITS, PH.D.

DAVID MOORE ROBINSON, PH.D., LL.D.

MODERN TRAITS
IN OLD GREEK LIFE

BY
CHARLES BURTON GULICK, A.M., Ph.D.

COOPER SQUARE PUBLISHERS, INC.
NEW YORK
1963

Published 1963 by Cooper Square Publishers, Inc.
59 Fourth Avenue, New York 3, N. Y.
Library of Congress Catalog Card No. 63-10291

PREFACE

MUCH new light has been thrown on the course of daily life in old Greece by the investigations of scholars in the last three decades. Besides increasing archaeological and epigraphical material, the papyri from Egypt have opened to view fresh stores of knowledge concerning the public and private life of Greeks in the Hellenistic period, from much of which interesting inferences can be drawn for the classical age.

The following pages are an attempt to show how far the manners and customs of ancient Hellas have left their mark on the routine of our modern daily life. It does not pretend to be a complete handbook of the subject, and the plan of the Series of which the book forms a part precludes the citation of authorities in learned notes. Nor can it do more than hint at the quality of that ineffable thing which we call the Greek spirit. All that is hoped is that the work may make clear the abounding vitality of ancient Greece in European and American life.

CHARLES BURTON GULICK

HARVARD UNIVERSITY
October, 1926

CONTENTS

CONTENTS

MODERN TRAITS IN
OLD GREEK LIFE

MODERN TRAITS IN
OLD GREEK LIFE

I. INTRODUCTION

WHEN we sit at a concert listening to a great violinist, we are often diverted by the flash of a large diamond on one of the fingers of his bow hand. If we like the music and the artist we dismiss the impression from our minds with the thought that it is merely a bit of personal vanity on the part of the player. But when we read that the practice of displaying handsome rings to the audience was in vogue at musical contests twenty-four hundred years ago, and learn that the eminent Greek lyre-players of the time of Timotheus wore jewels on the right hand — the hand which held the plectrum and sounded the strings — we find that we are confronting a long tradition of professional practice. Perhaps this persistent habit may be traceable to the Greek desire to discover and reveal beauty everywhere, and to harmonize glints of color

[3]

with musical tones, if such a combination is possible. Granting that this was the aim of the Greek artist, we must then be dealing not merely with the momentary whim of a vain musician, but with traits of Greek character which are also human showing themselves in similar guise wherever similar situations occur, and persisting, therefore, through long years in the practices of a guild.

In the following pages, wherein some facts are set forth relating to the conduct of daily life among the Greeks of classical times, it is not maintained, of course, that all such resemblances as we note in the life of today are the result of direct borrowing from the Greeks. What we practice still under the force of tradition — and great is its power — is of twofold origin: we are still faithful, for better or for worse, to the usages of our common Indo-European ancestors and our tribal and racial forebears; and we still carry on some of the thought and customs of the Greeks, either taken directly from their literature and life or transmitted through the Romans and the civilization of Western Europe. In many cases it would be difficult to point to a Greek source without a Roman intermediary.

[4]

Many persons today think that the proud results of modern thought and knowledge have nearly, if not quite, obliterated all these influences, and especially those which have flowed from the Greek, and that the Greeks have no lessons to teach us now; and it is true that we do many things that are not Greek, or that are not done in the Greek way. Nevertheless there has scarcely been an age, since the decline of the Greek schools in the West, which has been summoned to face more squarely the same universal and fundamental problems of life which engaged the best poetry and philosophy of the Greeks. And never has an age called for the same intellectual and spiritual stamina which was theirs as does our own. The greater our material progress, the more imminent becomes the danger of missing what the Greeks persistently saw, — undying realities behind the presentations of sense, belief in which moulded and guided their way of life throughout the best period of their history.

Every period of European culture which has drawn its own sustenance from the classical mind has been followed by a period of decay and transition in which that nurture has been neglected or rejected. We are just at the end of such a transition now, and the mistakes of this neglect in our generation are coming to be recognized. The evolutionary method of science and history, teaching as it does the immense importance of origins, is beginning to turn men back to the Greek fountainhead of all ideas. One may question whether the ideas about life entertained by Germans and Americans, Russians and Frenchmen, would be intelligible to each other in any sense were it not for the common medium afforded by their Greek inheritance. What is now needed, beside the understanding of our debt to Greece and Rome, is the faculty to draw for our own inspiration upon the experience of the Greeks, and above all the will to evoke that spiritual vision which was theirs. So powerfully and directly has the stream of Greek influence flowed upon European life, so unconsciously have its smallest currents filtered into the roots of our own life, that even where Greek influence seems remote, it is safer to allege that it is there in doubtful cases. Certain it is that even in the heterogeneous composition of America, it is not India, nor Palestine, even, nor China, nor Africa, nor any other region where ancient peoples have attained high culture, but Greece, and Greece aided by Rome, that has given character to our daily life. One of the greatest of modern scholars and teachers, Thaddeus Zielinski, has said: [1] "All of us have two Fatherlands, — the one is the land from which we take our name, the other is antiquity. In body and soul, we belong to our own country; in spirit, however, we are, or should be, one with the great past." Or as the poet Shelley maintained: "We are all Greeks. Our laws, our literature, our religion, our arts, have their root in Greece." We are, therefore, nearer in thought to the Greeks of ancient times than to many contemporary nations.

To understand our relation and debt to Greece we must distinguish between the actual copying of Greek life and thought on the one hand, and that unconscious possession of habits and thoughts which go back historically to Greece; between the attitude of imitation of things Greek as a rigid and sterile norm, and the saner recognition of Greece as the germ and seed of all that is best in life today. The first can be seen in those periods of literary history which have produced the 'pseudo-

classic; ' the second is all about us, all the
time — sometimes recognized, sometimes not,
but as certain, as inevitable, as necessary, as
our physical ancestry.

One may illustrate the nature of the prob-
lem we have set before us from language itself.
We have coincidence and accidental similarities on the one hand, and on the other, direct
and conscious derivation from the Greek. Bits
of American slang, which can by no possibility
be translations of the Greek, show the same
mental processes working to attain certain
forms of speech. The Greek, like the American,
could say, " It is up to you," " He will get
all that is coming to him; " and when he wished
to approve the remark of another, " You said
something " came readily to his lips. These,
however, are chance similarities, and weigh
little when compared with the rich vocabulary
of indispensable words which our English language has taken over from the Greek.
' Church ' and ' theatre,' ' cypress ' and ' quince,'
' asparagus ' and ' peach,' ' idea ' and ' phrase,'
' psychiatry ' and ' heliotherapy,' are a few
words chosen at random from the Greek store-
house without which our language would be
poor indeed. ' Butter,' a thing which the Greeks

[8]

did not esteem, is nevertheless a Greek word. Even differences in dialect have left their traces here and there in English words. For example, any clever contrivance was called a *mêchanê* by the Ionians and Athenians, a *mâchanâ,* with a broad *a,* by the Dorians. The latter carried the word to Southern Italy, where the Romans heard it and borrowed it with only slight change, *mâchina.* Through this divergence, itself the interesting reflexion of important ethnological movements, our language was enriched by two sets of words represented by ' machine ' and ' mechanic.'

Since Roman times every age has drawn what it desired, what was most suited to its new conditions and congenial to its spirit, from the culture of the Greeks. Far from exhausting itself, the spring of Greek life and literature and language still flows in fresh rills through the wide reaches of modern life. The science of classical philology today is more interesting and instructive than it has ever been before. In view of our dependence upon the Greek, it is nonsense to say of anything which is unintelligible, " That is all Greek to me." Since most words expressive of our higher culture and science are Greek or Latin, we should fail

to be intelligible in ordinary daily intercourse if we did not use Greek and Latin
derivatives.

Much may be learned of ancient life from
the manners and customs of the modern Hel-
lenes, as well as from a study of ancient books
and monuments of art. In them we see a
people thoroughly of our own times in their
education and aspiration, yet but slightly
touched by the feudalism and capitalism of the
western world. Survivals of old practices in
trade, in family conventions, in legends, even
in religion, bind the people of modern Hellas
to their past. The land they live in, its geolog-
ical, botanical, and meteorological features, are
reflected in their habits of thought today as
they were reflected in their ancient literature.
The keen-eyed observation of a people who
lived always on the most intimate terms with
nature expressed itself with extraordinary full-
ness and clearness. The Greeks today have a
saying that when God said " Let there be
light," He added " And let it shine with greatest brightness in Greece." And indeed much
of the serenity and clarity of Greek thought
may be the result of the strong lights of
Greek landscape, where, at least in Attica, the

centre of intellectual achievement, fogs are uncommon, and where the misty half-light of northern skies rarely obscured their clear-eyed vision of reality. In the region about Athens today there are scarcely a half-dozen totally cloudy days in the whole year.

Mountain and sea together determined many features of Greek life. The sea pierces deep into the land, the mountains rise high above the sea. The sea made for communication, for growth in knowledge and influence; it has always been the great carrier of civilization. The mountain tended to divide settlements into isolated cantons, to foster seclusion and independence, but also to make life harder. Ruskin, in *Modern Painters,* has dwelt with some exaggeration, it must be admitted, on the Greek dislike of mountains. But the Anglo-Saxons also disliked them. Mountains are hard, they are stormy, some of them lie restlessly over the bodies of angry giants, who cause avalanches, volcanic outbursts, devastating torrents. Yet Pan dwelt there among them, and Pan could protect his own Greeks against the Persians. The mountains crowded out fertile valleys, and living among them was precarious; but they also crowded out unwelcome invaders, and thus became the defenders and sponsors of tribes proud of their long-seated possession, haughty with aristocratic seclusion, deep-rooted in their conservatism and love of tradition.

Greek culture, by which we mean generally Ionian and Athenian culture, was bred in an area amazingly small. The intellectual forces which arose on Greek soil and later penetrated through the western world got their impetus from the genius of a few men, bred almost like exotics in the narrow limits of the ancient city-state, shut within walled towns, travelling only with difficulty, putting to sea cautiously only when the weather most favored their light craft, all classes rubbing shoulder to shoulder in a contact of differing social elements more intimate and inevitable than any which the world has ever seen since. The more we try to realize and explain the Greek genius and its influence on the world, both west and east, the greater appears the discrepancy between that influence and the meagre material resources which the Greeks possessed. Attica, the country of the Athenians, was less than one-tenth the size of Massachusetts. Its population could not have numbered in the prosperous fifth century more than half a million people, and may have been much less. The entire land of Hellas could be contained twelve times within the boundaries of Texas.

II. IN THE HOME

1. THE DWELLING

SIMPLICITY marked the lives of all Greeks in the classical era. In the East, to be sure, in Ionia and in Lesbos, some portion of the riches of Asia, the luxury of Lydia and of Persia, were shared by the thin line of Greek cities which were planted on the narrow coast. Ephesus, Miletus, Smyrna — terminals of caravan routes from the interior, ports of entry from the seas for ages — might boast comparative comfort. But on the mainland, at the southern extremity of the Balkan peninsula, the simple, even scanty food, the poor houses, the furniture only slightly ornamented, and the clothing, all excited the ridicule of the rich Persians. Cold, hunger, and discomfort must often have been the daily portion of the people whose collective genius, in spite of it all, gave to the modern world its rich treasure of ideas.

Not until the fourth century before Christ did Hellenic civilization begin to show any refinements of comfort in daily life, and this change coincided with the gradual withdrawal of the ordinary citizen from public life. There came a greater reluctance to perform military service, a corresponding growth in commercial and industrial activity, a retirement from the popular assembly and law courts to the seclusion of home. Yet at no time can Athens be thought of as enjoying a luxury comparable to that of Rome in the days of Nero.

In the classical era, we are told, one could not have distinguished the house of the most eminent citizen from that of the humblest day-laborer. Themistocles and Aristeides, one rich, the other poor, alike lived in houses which the American workman would disdain.

Their houses, to be sure, had long since outgrown the form inherited from the tent of our common Indo-European ancestors — the round huts which we find imitated at Mycenae in the circular tombs with pointed roof. In shape they had become rectangular or square, the country house retaining more faithfully the traditions of the Homeric house, whereas the town dwelling developed individual features according to its position in a street or

block, or the needs of the tenant. Under the
sloping gables of a countryman's house was
contained a square space divided on the sides
into stalls for animals and small rooms for
slaves, beyond which were the somewhat
larger rooms, with ' the best room ' in the middle. Often there was a second story. This type
occurs in other parts of Europe, and is very
old.

The city house, in spite of occasional varia-
tion in detail, retained in its main lines the
same character for many centuries. Presenting to the street a wall pierced only by a
narrow door and one or two small windows,
generally high above the street, it received
light from the inner court. For the city streets
were narrow, sometimes not more than fifteen
feet wide, so that at one period a special tax
was imposed on the owner whose street door
opened outward. Round the court, which often
took up half the ground space of the dwelling,
were grouped rooms and an alcove. It was,
and is, a house especially adapted to a southern climate, and survives in the so-called
' Pompeian ' architecture of today, wherein a
court, loggia, or pergola are reminiscent of the
ancient court and of the ancient preference

for life out of doors rather than under a dark roof.

But the American of today, accustomed on entering a house to catch glimpses of many rooms with doors opening upon a hall and staircase, would find in the Greek house, as in most European houses, a certain privacy and reticence which he would not understand. In no Greek house was the staircase a structural part of the edifice; a ladder, or at best narrow steep stairs, led up from some remote room to the upper floor. He would find the chambers dark and disconnected, except through the court, for light and warmth are not so important in the climate of Greece as they are in our northern cities. In the better houses, if the surly porter admitted him, he would come either at once, or through a vestibule, into the court, whence he would see, behind the columns which lined the court, corridors on which opened small rooms for the housing and the work of the slaves; facing the south, an open recess or sun-parlor in which much of the family life went on; and beyond, or at one side of this, a large room, or 'men's hall.' The private rooms of the women were either on the farthest side of the court or in the second story. While no pious Greek would have thought for a moment of competing with the splendor of a temple, nevertheless his dwelling-house, thus gradually evolved from the conglomeration of buildings which formed a Homeric palace, was reminiscent of the threefold divisions of a temple: the fore hall, or vestibule, recalls the fore-temple, or *pronaos;* the court, with its recess or alcove, is like the sanctuary, or cella, containing the altar to Zeus, ' god of the enclosure '; beyond that, the private rooms of master and mistress, with the great chest containing their most prized heirlooms and other valuables, corresponds to the *opisthodomos,* or treasure room of the temple.

This is the type found at Priene, on the coast of Asia Minor, where houses of the fourth and third centuries before Christ remain in a fair state of preservation. There are no houses of this period as yet uncovered in Athens. On the island of Delos, the houses of the third and second centuries show a later improvement of the court, in which columns often surround it on all four sides, thus producing a complete peristyle, such as later is to be found in the rear of a Roman house. But wherever we find the Greek house, we are impressed by the arrangements made for the seclusion of the women. Only occasionally might a passer-by see through the outer door a group of women and children in the alcove across the court.

There was no running water in the Greek house. It had to be brought daily by slaves, or in early times, by the daughters of the household, from a public spring or fountain. The tyrant Peisistratus, in the sixth century, improved and increased the supply by conduits laid from springs in the neighboring mountains; but the water of Athens was never esteemed so highly as that of Corinth or Thebes or Pergamum.

The ground floor of the house was simply the original earth beaten hard or strewn with pebbles. Later, the floors were paved with flag-stones or with mosaic. Mats and rugs were essential, and in the Periclean age the importation of rare and expensive rugs from the East became common.

2. THE FURNITURE

AFTER the fifth century the artistic impulse of the Greeks led them to add tasteful decoration to the bare walls of the court and the inner rooms excepting the dining-room, where the smoke of the fire was likely to blacken the walls and ceiling; and from the earliest times, the house furniture was both comfortable and ornate among the more prosperous classes. Unfortunately, we can form at best only remote conjectures regarding the beauty of color and design in mural decorations, now lost, from the vase-paintings of the fifth and fourth centuries, and from the later houses of Delos and Pompeii. From these we may assume that the walls were divided laterally into wainscoting, panel, and frieze. The panels were square or rectangular; the frieze was often ornamented with stucco or terra-cotta reliefs, small but effective. But concerning the furniture we know more. Here beauty and usefulness were combined with practical sense and artistic fancy. Images of the family gods and of the gods of the state filled niches in most of the rooms; a small altar to Zeus adorned the court and was used for the family sacrifices. Small household shrines, sometimes grotesque on the outside, would be found, when the outer doors were opened, to contain exquisite statuettes of gods and goddesses.

Beside the walls were set the chests used instead of our bureaus, and these often served conveniently as benches.

In the sleeping-rooms, and even elsewhere, were couches of handsome wood, often inlaid with ivory or gold and silver, and these, bolstered with embroidered cushions, were used at dinners, and for reading and writing. On them the dead were carried to the grave. The couch survives today in the couch, divan, lounge, or 'chaise longue' of our houses. It lacked the high board or posts at the head and foot of the modern bed, but like the colonial four-poster, it was often adorned with a linen or woolen valance round the bottom. In Homeric times, it was piled high with rugs to make it soft. Later, mattresses came into use, stuffed with vegetable pods, wool, or feathers, and covered with embroidered spreads of wool, but probably not with sheets.

The chairs were of three types: there was the stool, without arms or back, used by men and women at work; the chair with reclining back, used especially by women at work or at rest; and the chair of state, or *thronos, cathedra,* which was solid and heavy, having back and arms, and not so common in private houses as in the palace or the public portico, or in the gymnasium where philosophers talked and taught, and in the stadium where the judges formally gave decisions in the games. It often required a footstool for comfort, and was spread with a handsomely woven cloth or cushion. The uses of the *cathedra,* from which, through the French, comes the English word ' chair,' are reflected today whenever we speak of a professor holding the chair of philosophy or of Greek, or of a ' chairman ' presiding at a committee meeting, or when we speak of a judgment or dictum uttered *ex cathedra, i.e.,* officially and authoritatively; or when we build a *cathedral,* wherein the bishop has his throne and holds his ' see ' (*sedes*).

Tables were used mostly at meals, for which they were brought in and set beside the couches on which the guests reclined, two or three together. For this purpose, the tables stood lower than the couches. But they were of extraordinary variety in shape and pattern. One favorite form was the tripod, usually of bronze. The tables of the Hellenistic period show round tops of marble or costly wood, especially the fragrant cedar; or rectangular tops suitable for the display of handsome vases and other valuables.

Gas and electricity have so improved the lighting facilities of mankind since the nineteenth century that only the enforced use of a candle or oil lamp today can give us any idea of the difficulties which beset the ancients at night. In Homeric palaces the servants brought in torches of pitch-pine, and these were often used even in the later periods. Later, wooden splints soaked in olive oil and bound with metal ferrules served to give a steadier light. In the classical period we hear of earthenware and bronze lamps, small, shallow vessels containing olive oil, with one or more holes for wicks, and in the fifth century, B.C., imported Etruscan candelabra began to add both light and ornament to the room. Nevertheless reading at night was difficult, and ' burning the midnight oil ' as an expression describing an assiduous student, may be traced back to this era. During the hard times of the Peloponnesian War, oil became dear, and the miserly householder accordingly objected when a slave put too large a wick into the evening lamp. Tallow and wax candles seem to have come much later from the Etruscans.

Nothing corresponding to the American method of heating houses from a central fire was known before Roman times. The Greek house had its fireplace, which, however, was apt to shed smoke to such a degree that it was customary to leave the walls and ceiling of the room in which it was placed unadorned with reliefs or paintings. Open braziers, containing a small fire of charcoal, afforded a scanty local warmth. The conditions in a farmhouse in America or in most of the older houses in Europe, as regards heat, resemble those to be found in an ordinary Greek house, ancient and modern. One must go outdoors to get warm. The Cynic Diogenes had but one request to make of Alexander the Great, and that was to get out of his sunlight; and the phrase, " a place in the sun," is a reminiscence of the ancient struggle for warmth.

Whatever imperfections and inadequacies we may have found in the household furniture of the Greeks were counterbalanced by the beauty and variety of their vessels of earthenware, of bronze, and even of precious metals; later, of glass paste or faience. The inventive and artistic genius of potter, metal-worker, and vase-painter found expression in almost inconceivable variety. The Romans either imported Greek jars and dishes directly, or imitated them consciously, so that some of the most beautiful forms of pitcher, vase, bowl, and cup are today a part of our Greek inheritance.

In all the material refinements and conveniences of the modern household, the Greek has been the leader and teacher, and has furnished the best patterns. He first embodied the enterprise and inventiveness of Europe and America; he is the first Westerner. He required a comfortable chair; the Oriental does not. The contrast between the elaborate furnishings of the American house and the meagre appointments of a Japanese house is directly due to the example of the Greeks.

3. The Apparel

WHEN we study their clothing, it seems at first harder to justify the claims of Greek influence on modern fashion; differences of climate, of taste, of materials have naturally produced differences in modes, and fashions changed in ancient times almost as fast as

[25]

they do today. Yet even here, the Greek tradition may be seen in certain garments. Certainly in the case of men's dress we see in the Greeks a preference for practical convenience over the stiff Oriental magnificence which prevailed before the defeat of Persia. After Alexander's conquests Oriental influences came in afresh, but they are noticeable chiefly in the dress of women.

" Man," says Carlyle, " is by nature a *Naked Animal*." But with civilization, or if you prefer, with the knowledge of good and evil, came some kind of clothing, and with clothing some kind of pouch, pocket, or wallet; for man is a marsupial animal. And so, in the case of the Greeks, although they stood closer to nature than we moderns do, only a slavish dependence upon the testimony of the vase-paintings could lead us to infer that the Greeks discarded clothing as freely as these works of art seem to show, except, of course, in the case of athletes and of workmen toiling before a hot fire. To be sure, the Greek looked with ridicule on the trousers of the Persian and the breeches of the Celt. The man of Athens wore no stockings, and on a campaign in the cold north he was obliged to wrap all sorts of coverings round his legs, unless he had the endurance of Socrates, who, like children in Canada nowadays, could walk barefoot on the ice without discomfort or complaint. But the adult engaged in the business of the market, the assembly, or the courts associated dignity with modesty, and was as careful about the proper adjustment of his cloak as any man of today can be.

In the earliest period, men wore a long linen robe, unbelted, which sometimes reached to the feet. This is called the Ionic *chiton* (*tunica*), and was of Eastern origin. Wide sleeves reached to the elbows. After the Persian wars, the Doric chiton of wool came into style. This reached only to the knee, was belted round the waist, and had no sleeves. It was fastened by pins or brooches at the shoulders. Workmen often loosed the fastening on the right, so that the right arm and shoulder were entirely free and bare.

In the street, men wore as outer garment a long rectangular piece of wool, draped gracefully in large folds round the back and arms, and giving and requiring at once a certain dignity of carriage. Younger men, and especially men on horseback and travellers, pre-

[27]

ferred the riders' cloak or cape slung over the chiton.

From the earliest times, reflected in the Homeric poems, down to our own, the dress of women has differed from the dress of men both in form and in greater liberty of ornamentation. In Homer, women wear a long woolen *peplos*, which in time was discarded for the linen chiton. The folds are voluminous and graceful. The neck and arms, except in the Ionic chiton, are left bare. A shawl or heavy veil sometimes covers the head and back. A girdle of gold, silver, or linen handsomely embroidered, gave variety of lines, according to whether it was placed just below the breast, or allowed to hang more loosely round the hips.

In Homer's time, men wore their hair long, a custom later retained by the Spartans, and by priests of the Greek church today. They also allowed the beard to grow. Alexander the Great, like American officers today, compelled his soldiers to shave; but a moustache without a beard was the mark of a northern barbarian. Women arranged their long hair — only the courtesan ' bobbed ' it — in a great variety of ways, but in general so as to give the effect of naturalness and also to narrow the forehead. They added numerous ornaments, such as diadems of rich textiles or metals; ribbons, kerchiefs, or plates of tortoise-shell, or silver held the back hair in place. Crowns of flowers, or of gold and silver leaf were worn even by men, sometimes as a badge of office or in public. speaking, and often as a sign of victory in battle or in games, or at sacrifices and public festivals.

A Greek seldom wore a hat. On a long journey he might for protection against the sun don the Thessalian *petasos,* with low crown and wide brim, precursor of the ' sailor hat.' Fastened by a cord round the chin, it was often allowed to fall back and lie upon the shoulders. Workmen, especially those engaged before a hot fire, wore a close fitting felt, without brim, which survives in the fez of today in the Near East. A variety with loose top which fell forward, and usually to be found in the East, became the well-known ' liberty cap ' of our Revolutionary times. Women preferred veils or shawls to hats, but after Alexander's time, they occasionally wore a kind of straw hat with very high and pointed crown.

Before the Greeks attained the luxury of the Hellenistic Age, they regarded shoes and sandals as only a little more essential than hats. Nevertheless, they were manufactured, especially at Athens and in the East, in great variety. The slippers and sandals of the women took on great beauty of ornament in embroidery, as did the high boots worn by hunters and riders. Certain colors became a sign of rank or office; the gymnasium-master wore white shoes.

Gold ornaments were affected mostly by women, as in Western Europe today. Ear-rings, rings for the hair, necklaces, bracelets, arm-bands, combs, and pins testify to the artistic skill of the goldsmith. But men wore only a ring, the stone of which was cut in intaglio; the bezel surrounding it often bore an inscription, so that the whole formed a seal easily carried about. Men also liked to carry a staff, long and with a crook at the top, surviving today in the shepherd's crook and the ecclesiastical crozier. Yet often it was surmounted by a carved head or flower, and from earliest times this was the badge of envoys, heralds, public speakers, and all others in authority, permanent or temporary. It became the sceptre of

kings, and in art it is often portrayed in the
hands of the gods. Women carried sunshades,
men never, except in the spirit of burlesque.
Women frequently carried fans of palm leaves
or thin strips of wood, and in their rooms they
kept a supply of hand mirrors of bronze or
silver. Sometimes the bronze is overlaid with
a thin layer of silver, presenting a better re-
flecting surface. In any case they had to be
protected against scratching or tarnishing. Two
varieties well-known in the latter part of the
fifth century have their counterparts today.
One is the disc mounted on a handle; the other
is double, without handles, but hinged together so that when opened at right angles,
like the glass in a vanity-case, they reflected
two images. The women of Athens, paler than
other women because they lived so much in-
doors, used cosmetics, white lead and rouge,
and touched up their eyebrows with a metallic
stain imported from Egypt. These materials
were kept in beautifully wrought receptacles
of boxwood (*pyx,* compare English *box*),
earthenware, or metal. False hair became one
of the affectations introduced in the Hellenistic period. It may be said, however, that the
Athenian women, and still more the Dorian

women, never carried the art of make-up as far as the women of Rome, nor did they, like the Romans and the women of the eighteenth century, wear patches.

4. THE FOOD

IF " the apparel oft proclaims the man," the quantity and quality of his food are apt to mark his character quite as well; and the simplicity and frugality of the Greeks in their best period are plainly attested in what they ate. " Tell me what you eat," said the gourmet Brillat-Savarin, " and I will tell you what you are." The Persians, who according to Herodotus were in the habit of roasting whole oxen, horses, camels, and asses in extravagant barbecues, regarded Greek fare as poor and scant, and the luxurious Romans of Juvenal's day had only contempt for "the hungry little Greek." Yet the Greek tradition of abstemiousness and the temperance preached first by Socrates, and later emphasized by Plato and Aristotle, have lasted on through the ages in the Church, which makes gluttony one of the seven deadly sins. Socrates was no ascetic, at least in the mediaeval sense, but he constantly warns his hearers that overeating ruins souls as well as stomachs. " Bad men," he said, " live to eat and drink, good men eat and drink to live;" and to a friend who complained that he had no appetite he once said, " Acoumenos, the physician, has an excellent prescription for that: ' Don't eat.' "

> " *The fool that eats till he is sick*
> *must fast till he is well.*"

Of course the nature of Greek food was at first conditioned by the climate and soil of Greece itself. It is true that Pericles boasted, at the end of his career, that Athenian commercial and maritime relations were so widely extended that the port of the Peiraeus received large quantities of products from all sorts of countries, so that what was ordinarily found but rarely in other cities was enjoyed by Athenians in abundance and variety. But the habit of plain living inherited from simple ancestors persisted even in the later period, and is a marked characteristic of the Greeks of our time. The small variety of food available to the Homeric Greeks is remarked by Plato, who has much to say about food, never in quite the spirit of a thorough-going asceticism, but in the temper rather of a wise physician. He notices that the Greeks of the *Iliad* and *Odyssey* never boiled their meat; they ate no fish, or very little of it, and they had none of the relishes or sweets known to the Athenian cooks. A raw onion might accompany a cup of wine, exactly as the Greek peasant offers the two together to a traveller today. A poor sort of chick-peas or beans, dried, ground into flour, and eaten as a porridge, was the daily meal of the poor; but on festival occasions they got their share of the meat roasted and carefully turned on the spit, — beef, pork, mutton, and goat. In the use of the goat for food the northerner in Europe and America parts company with the Mediterranean southerner; we have no special word for goat's meat, as we have for calf's meat or veal, steer's meat or beef, pig's meat or pork — words on the use of which every one will remember the amusing and instructive passage in *Ivanhoe*. On the other hand, we generally abstain from horse meat, in spite of the fact that our Anglo-Saxon ancestors ate it, simply because the meats sanctioned by early Christianity corresponded largely with those which Pagan Greeks ate at sacrifices, and among these horses were not included by most Greeks.

With all the lack of variety, Homeric Greeks show valiant appetites. The housekeeper in the *Odyssey* — " the poem of eating " — " lavishes it from her store." And Homeric etiquette may be observed in the phrase " equal feast," which is constantly repeated. Every social worker today among the children of the poor knows that the teaching of good manners is most convincingly based on the principle of a fair share for all; a square deal and a square meal dwell not so far apart.

Bread, the gift of golden Demeter, has always been the food most highly esteemed by races which have emerged from barbarism. In many a symbol it is the staff of life — " men's marrow," the Greeks called it — the mainstay of life and the basis of all nourishment and growth. It is said that savages do not make bread; appropriately, therefore, the Greek mythology associated Demeter, giver of grain, with other gifts of civilization, — settled communities and laws to govern them, marriage and the sober virtues of domestic life. So strong was this belief in a logical connection between breadstuffs and a more orderly society that it expanded into a great conviction that country life was morally healthier and sounder than life in the city. " God the first garden made, and the first city Cain." Socrates cherished no illusion of that sort. He preferred life in the city. Living at a time when thinkers were urging that the proper study of mankind is man, he found his material for ethical study more conveniently at hand within the walls of Athens and the Peiraeus. " The woods and the fields," he tells Phaedrus, " can teach me no lessons; I get my instruction from men."

Some Greeks enjoyed richer food than others. The fertile plains of Thessaly, the watered lowlands of Boeotia, furnished greater variety than the thin soil of Attica or the stern régime of the Spartans commonly allowed. The Corinthians, too, who controlled the routes of trade which crossed at the Corinthian Gulf, were noted for luxurious living; but it was in Sicily and Magna Graecia that cookery became a fine art. Here were the first celebrated *chefs* of Europe, and from here came the first cook-books.[2] The Sicilian cook forms one of the typical characters of comedy, and Heracles, whose labors took him to Sicily, became the stock glutton of the Athenian stage. But his appearance in this character only emphasizes the Athenian contempt for over-eating. Heracles and the professional boxer, alike in the Athenian view of them, were thick-witted, because they ate too much, especially meat. The Greek would have understood Sir Andrew Aguecheek when he confessed: " I am a great eater of beef, and I believe that does harm to my wit."

Bread, then, constituted the chief diet of the Athenian and the Spartan. The poor had the simple cake of barley meal, pounded, parched, and mixed with oil or wine. Cheese made from the milk of goats or sheep added savor and a proper balance to this plain viand. The rich enjoyed the finer loaf of white bread, made with yeast, and sold at bake-shops, for which Athens was famous. The fancy of the cooks later produced moulds from which were formed loaves in many shapes, representing animal or geometric forms analogous to the stamped Eucharistic bread of the Greek church, or to the animal crackers given to our children. It is doubtful whether rice was known to the Greeks in the classical age. Rice and milk, made into a kind of pudding, and one of the commonest of Greek desserts today, is first mentioned in Byzantine times. Oats were known only as a weed, and rye-bread was not in favor.

Of green vegetables there was a great lack, still felt by the American who travels in Europe today. Various cresses and herbs, like thyme, which was regarded as the poor man's seasoning, and lettuce, parsley, and chervil find mention in the literature. Beans, peas, lentils, and lupines were common leguminous plants sold in the city, and mushrooms and artichokes were to be had in the country. But onions, garlic, leeks, and scallions ('the onion of Ascalon') were the commonest vegetables, to which were added occasionally the bulb of an edible iris still eaten by the Greek peasant, and beets and cucumbers. But the ancient and the mediaeval world knew not the potato, without which it would be hard to supply sufficient food in modern times.

Of fruits the Greeks had olives — preserved in oil, not brine — figs, grapes (especially raisins), dates, quinces, and undeveloped varieties of the apple and the pear. No American plum pudding or mince pie would be complete without the small raisins from Corinth which we call 'currants,' after the name of the district from which they come. Cherries (another

Greek word) came in from the East in Alexandrian times, then plums or damsons (named from Damascus), and peaches (named from Persia). But oranges and lemons, the commonest of fruits in Greece today, seem to have been unknown as food, unless the mythical golden apples of the Hesperides were oranges; the Greeks still call them *portogallia* (from Portugal), as the Germans call them *apfelsine* (*i.e.*, apples from Messina).

The favorite nuts were the almond and an edible acorn which is still produced abundantly in Peloponnesus; also the pine-nut, a small and delicious variety which, under the name of piñon or pignola, has recently found its way to the American market and is grown in California. Walnuts and chestnuts seem to have been imported into Greece, where they are abundant today, in Xenophon's time.

The boiling of meat, especially pork and lamb, quite unknown in Homer, became common in the classical period. But the poor scarcely tasted the meat of large animals except at the state festivals, when it was roasted on the altars and eaten immediately by the participants, or, if no special prohibition enjoined by the ritual forbade, it was distributed among the butchers and sold ready-cooked at their booths. Often, of course, the hunters brought in venison and wild boar from the mountain, or trappers managed to get wild duck, partridge, wood pigeon, quail, thrushes, and blackbirds. Tame geese are mentioned by Homer, and goose's liver (*pâté de fois gras*) became a luxury of the later time. The cock and the hen — " Persian birds " they were called — are first mentioned in Greece in the sixth century B.C.

The Athenian, as distinguished from the Homeric Greek, ate fish with avidity. The deep bays along the coast provided fish more cheaply than meat could be raised, and tunny, sturgeon, herring, mullet, anchovies, sprats, and polyps (squid) were the favorite of all classes. Occasionally the rich might purchase shell-fish of the sorts known today — oysters, scallops, crabs, and lobsters.

All cooking, as in the Mediterranean countries today, was done with oil, and flavoring was added with herbs, cheese, and salt (obtained from sea-water); but pepper, mustard, and spices belong to the period when Alexander's conquests had opened highways of commerce to the East.

Wine was the chief, in fact almost the only drink used in antiquity. The milk of goats and sheep was drunk in the country, and it was employed in various culinary uses in the city. Turned into cheese, it was a favorite food everywhere. Cow's milk was never in common use, for the Greeks had the same difficulties in the treatment of larger cattle and in coaxing the cow to yield her milk which the traveller observes in southern countries today. The calf was not taken away from the cow immediately after birth, so that only a small quantity of milk was available for the herdsman.

The most highly esteemed wine, " the blood of Scio's vine," came to Athens from the island of Chios; and in general the islands yielded better varieties than the soil of Attica could produce. In some parts of Greece wine was mixed with resin to correct acidity, producing the " retzinato " so common among the modern Greeks. The pine-cone which surmounts the wand of Dionysus and his revellers may perhaps be the symbol of this early practice of the vintners. Aromatic herbs, also, and juniper berries, mastic, rose petals, wormwood, and hyssop were frequently steeped in wine to produce potions used mostly by physicians. But the latter, as early as the fifth century, were beginning to restrict the use of wine for medicinal purposes. Otherwise, neither law nor custom, other than that dictated by common decency, intervened to prevent wine-drinking. A bowl of wine was part of the regular ration supplied to boys in the Cretan mess. Spartan babies were dipped in wine to make them strong. Women and slaves, unlike those of Rome, were free to drink their share.

Plato, in the fourth century, would forbid wine to boys under eighteen, and he would have liked to see it used by no man under thirty; Montaigne said forty. But the natural inclination of the Greek toward moderation in drinking as in eating, and the practice of diluting the wine with water, freed the Greeks from any charge of intemperance, — a charge which no one but the strictest ascetic would be inclined to bring against them. The Greeks are a temperate, though wine-drinking, people today. Drunkenness is exceedingly rare, as it was rare in antiquity except in the Dionysiac revel, when it was neither a sin against the gods nor a crime against the State; and even here it is possible to outweigh the exaggerations of the comic poets with examples of soberness furnished, to cite a few cases at random, by Socrates, — a hearty drinker, but never a drunkard, — Euripides, Phocion, and Demosthenes.

Civilization has tended to postpone the chief meal of the day from an earlier to a later hour. So, in the Homeric poems, we read of the three meals, breakfast, dinner, supper; but in the busy Athens of the fifth century the meals are breakfast, luncheon, dinner. The first of these has at all times been a slight affair for the Greek. In ancient times a piece of bread or a barley cake dipped in wine sufficed, as in modern times a small cup of coffee with or without bread. Luncheon, eaten a little before noon, was somewhat heartier, but not so abundant as to spoil the afternoon exercise in palaestra or gymnasium. The master of the house reclined on a couch; the women and children, including boys under eighteen, sat at the master's feet or on chairs of their own.

The principal meal was eaten at sun-down; and this, in the life of the men especially, became the centre and the occasion of many social gatherings, the intellectual character of which is echoed in the newspaper " Symposium." From Plato to Athenaeus, or through more than six hundred years, symposium, or "banquet," was a favorite title for discussions, dialogues, and debates, and as such is still well-known in our popular literature. Women and girls had no part in these; they were present only when the feast celebrated a wedding, mourned the death of a relative, or marked the bestowal of a name upon a new-born child.

Dinners were, in fact, the sole form of entertainment available in the evening. Even when the guests danced, as they frequently did according to Homer, the feast was the inspiration of the dancing. Balls and dances in the modern sense were unknown. The theatre, of course, was a day-time amusement, and restricted to the time of the Dionysiac festivals. Being the only resource of an evening, the dinner-party was seized upon as the excuse for every kind of entertainment. Not always a mere carouse and revel, it was accompanied by the playing of many sorts of games, among which the *kottabos* was for a time in fashion. In this a small metal figure, balanced on the top of a lamp-stand, was shot at with drops of wine flipped from the drinkers' cups until it fell upon a pan below. The manner of its fall, and the sound it made as it struck the pan, were held to be prophetic of the thrower's luck in love. From these simple amusements there came later the introduction of panto-mimes, — in which professional *hetaerae* broke through the restrictions which applied to re-spectable women, and made their first appear-ance in what may be called vaudeville. In con-nection with such a dinner a Sicilian showman, impresario of a small troupe of pantomime players, once anticipated the remark of P. T. Barnum, that " the public likes to be fooled." At the banquet, too, we hear of the guessing of riddles and conundrums, the performance of acrobats, jugglers, and marionette players, and the more serious discussions which Plato ideal-ized. One famous clown, Pantaleon, has lent his name (' Pantaloon ') as well as his art to many a Drury Lane spectacle.

A dinner given by a private host was con-ducted with pleasurable simplicity and spon-taneity. With entire absence of formality the host, as in Shakspere's time, bade his guests orally to the feast, or sent his servants with the invitation. A guest was entirely free to in-vite a friend to go with him. Naturally it was a mark of good manners to come at the appointed time, but there was no waiting for a belated guest, and the dinner might be later broken in upon by a party of revellers from another house.

Written invitations were issued in the more formal Ptolemaic and Roman periods. One of these, written on papyrus, reads: " So-and-so invites you to dine in the precinct of the Lord Serapis, tomorrow, the fifteenth, at the ninth hour." Even here the brief time allowed between the invitation and the party itself is in marked contrast to the long interval which modern observance of formality requires.

From the occasional dinner to the more permanent dining club transition was easy, and it was not long before the *eranos,* which in Homer was a kind of picnic, developed into an association of men, usually young, for the mutual benefit and entertainment of the group, or to further and maintain the worship of some divinity. The members contributed sums for the dinner to be held at the meeting, while one of their number provided the place, arranged for the services of a professional cook who was brought from the market-place, hired the flute-players, and attended to all other matters pertaining to the banquet. From such an association, in which a god was frequently revered as the common ancestor of the members, was soon evolved the idea and the practice of a benefit association. If, for example, one of the members was condemned by the State to pay a fine, the others contributed a share to make up the required sum; or if a member was captured in war, his ransom might be provided by the fellow members of his *eranos,* which thus became the prototype of modern benevolent and fraternal organizations, although the notion of insurance, in the sense of today, was probably absent.

Some of these clubs naturally departed from their exclusively social purpose and became, in the thickening strife of Athenian democracy, the centres of political activity and propaganda, often in the interest of oligarchical or reactionary parties. The young men of these clubs affected the dress and long hair of the Spartans, and were derided as ' Laconomaniacs.' More seriously, they were accused of many crimes and misdemeanors, ranging from the mutilation of the Hermae to the secret control of trials and elections — exactly the kind of recrimination often heard and believed today.

No Greek banquet or symposium could proceed without first pouring a libation to the gods, and each bowl of mixed wine, as it was brought in, was consecrated to them or to the " Good Spirit." Another Greek custom which has survived even more persistently than this ' grace before meat ' is the drinking of a health to friends present or absent; the toasts were proposed by the ' master of the symposium,' also sometimes called the ' king,' who was chosen from the guests by lot, unless the host preferred to exercise the office.

We have seen that the symposium prompted the use of a new literary form, the dialogue. It also gave rise to the pantomime, in which, as in Xenophon's *Symposium,* an action is portrayed by dancing and gestures, and to the mime, short pieces or plays, without chorus or plot — and thus distinct from ' legitimate ' tragedy and comedy — in which a few persons enact a realistic incident from daily life. These began in the fifth century with Sophron, of whose works Plato is said to have been a devoted reader; but they are best represented for us in the mimes of Herodas, written in the third century B.C., depicting genre scenes of life in Alexandria and elsewhere. The pantomime, well-known and delightfully practiced by

Europeans, never became a favorite form of art in America, unless the moving-pictures may be regarded as an offshoot of it. Its effect may be realized in witnessing such a work as " Die Puppenfée " of the Germans, or the Russian Ballet.

In connection with the banquet of the rich, we may notice the care which the Greeks of the better classes bestowed on the body. Even Socrates, whose poverty precluded frequent resort to a public bath, nevertheless observed the custom when invited to dinner at the poet Agathon's celebration. We speak of 'Turkish' baths today, but they are really Greek, having been introduced into Europe from Greek, Hellenistic, and Roman practice by the Persians and Arabs of later times. The large bathroom in the palace at Tiryns, with its floor made of a single limestone block weighing over twenty tons, carries the tradition back into Mycenaean times, and Greek athleticism maintained it in the historical period. Public baths were very common by the end of the fourth century B.C., and became a regular part of the pretentious gymnasia of Hellenistic times. The bather brought his own oil, strigil, and towels, but purchased such

[49]

substitutes for soap as were then known from the bath-tender, whose cheating propensities are noticed by Aristophanes. Soap is a northern invention and a Teutonic word descriptive of a washing agent first noticed among the ancient Belgians. In its place the Greeks used soda (which they called "nitre"), lye, and fuller's earth. Later a compound was invented which included honey, still often used for the skin. Vapor baths were the indulgence of the Sybarites, but Plato thought that only the aged and the ill should take warm baths. Still, warm baths were by no means a sign of decadence. They were known to the farmer-poet Hesiod, and they had the high sanction of Heracles, who refreshed himself, after his labors, in the hot springs of Sicily; and the Phaeacians, who represent a higher culture than that of Odysseus and his little island, revived him after many days of exertion with a warm bath. At all times the Greeks looked with scorn on people who neglected cleanliness. Of such they used to say: "They wash only thrice in a lifetime, — when they are born, when they marry, and when they die." We may recall Socrates' scrupulous care in bathing just before he drank the hemlock, " that we may not leave to the women the trouble of washing a dead body."

It is, therefore, not surprising that the bath-tub figures conspicuously in Greek art and letters, whereas in English literature, whether from prudery or from lack of use, it is not common before the nineteenth century.

5. THE FAMILY

GREEK institutions are largely permeated with the consciousness of the solidarity, if not the sacredness, of family life. It rested on the strong foundation of monogamy, recognized as the only proper relation in Homeric custom, and established as the only legal relation by later laws. The Achaean kings might carry on love affairs with other women, but even Aga-memnon had only one wife, Clytaemnestra; the Asiatic Priam had many. Here, again, Greek custom and law have set the standard for the western world. Whether in Sparta or in the Cretan laws of Gortyna, — in Athens or in Corinth or in Alexandria, — the binding character of family relationships, extending even to remote cousins, was recognized and affirmed. No crime was so great as the shed-ding of a parent's or a brother's blood; and

[51]

affection could be expressed in no higher terms than in the exercise of paternal, filial, and fraternal duty. The Greeks of today have inherited this consciousness of family obligation more conspicuously than any other nation of the West. In the theory and the practice alike of statecraft, the thought predominated that the community was an association of citizens all of whom were related by blood, all descended from a common ancestor. This, of course, was more marked in aristocratic communities, but even in democratic Athens the basis of the organization of state was the family, the clan, and the brotherhood (*phratry*).

This consciousness, this pride in the family, naturally affected the position of women, sometimes mitigating their rigid seclusion in Athens, sometimes enforcing it the more severely. Divorce was almost unknown, as in Greece today.

Yet the status of women varied with the place and the time. We must go to Homer for the best examples of conjugal affection and equality. The genial character of Homeric society, its frank joy of living, are reflected in the equal position of wife with husband. Odysseus and Penelope, Hector and Andromache,

[52]

call up scenes of tenderness, or right conduct between the married pair, which have
few parallels in other literatures. Equality is
assumed, not asserted; yet even in the more
favorable cases, we hear Hector admonishing
Andromache that her proper work is at the
loom, and Penelope and Arete reign within the
home, not outside. In the great poets of the
fifth and fourth centuries, however sympatheti-
cally they portray the lot of women, it is assumed, and sometimes stated, that " woman's
place is in the home." As Menander puts it:
" at the loom, not in the Assembly."

Something of the freedom accorded to
women in Homer's time may be observed later
in small, aristocratic cities like Sparta, where
girls as well as boys were trained in sports,
and women might dispose of their property
without the intermediation of a guardian. But
in Athens women lived secluded lives, which,
however, were by no means devoid of interest
and amusement. They had their own festivals
and also attended the greater festivals of the
State, like the Panathenaea and the Dionysia;
the latter included performances in the theatre.
Poetry and sculpture (especially the terra-
cottas and the grave-reliefs) attest the affec-

tion felt for wives, mothers, sisters, and nurses. But marriageable girls were surrounded with many safeguards which would be held intolerable today, and they saw their future husbands only at religious processions and sacrifices. Their seclusion may be explained in part by the great influx of foreigners into Athens in the Periclean Age, since conservative parents would be loath to expose their daughters to contact with aliens, most of whom were of the lower classes. Rarely was the right of intermarriage accorded to an alien. Married women went into the street attended by a slave woman or an elderly relative. Women of the *hetaera* class at this period were often noted for learning and wit as well as for beauty, and men of rank and probity, like Pericles and Socrates, treated them with respect.[3]

Three sanctions of family governance are recognized by Aristotle as axiomatic: the right of master over slave, the superiority of husband over wife, the power of father over children. Western civilization has abolished the first, has weakened the second, and seems in a fair way to abandon the third. The virtues of a wife, in the Greek view, were modesty, silence, obedience, and good housekeeping.

When seen in the street, we are told, the question about her should be, not " whose wife," but " whose mother is she? " Many ancient restrictions are still imposed by Greek society on women today, and even in England disabilities in regard to property and other rights attest the force of tradition.

With the depletion of men after the great Peloponnesian War (431–404),[4] with the necessity of earning a living thrust upon women as a result of that war, and, possibly because of the part played by women in nursing the wounded, their position gradually improved until, in the Hellenistic age, a decided emancipation is noticeable. In this period, Greece had lost her autonomy. Men retired more and more into the circle of home, and women came to own and manage more property. Rich women founded institutions for education and religion, and built notable monuments to their dead. The increase of education and opportunity for social intercourse afforded to respectable women at this time coincided with a corresponding lowering of the morals of the *hetaerae,* whose greed and looseness form the theme of later comedy. But it is never to be forgotten that long before, in the fifth century, Euripides prophesied the new time for the new woman, and the characters of noble womanhood which he draws stand out in convincing opposition to the scurrilous portraits of a comic poet like Aristophanes. Satire on women has always been part of the stock in trade of the comedian, and should not be understood too literally.

In the management of her household, which in the middle and upper classes included one or more slaves, and the care of her children in their earlier years, with spinning and weaving, sewing, embroidery, and cooking, the life of women seems on the whole to have been more industrious than that of men of their class. Clothes had to be washed by the river bank; but the dyeing and fulling of cloth fresh from the loom was done by men, and cooking rarely included the baking of bread, which was normally procured from the bakers.

Every woman of good family was under the guardianship of a man, who might be her father, eldest brother, uncle, or other nearest relative old enough to head the household; after marriage, her husband became her legal representative. A widow or orphan daughter with property must be immediately married after the death of husband or father, her guardian sometimes marrying her himself, or arranging for her marriage with his son or other close connection of the family. The object was to retain her property within the family.

6. MARRIAGE

ROUND the marriage ceremony clustered many traditions of religion and family practice, and some of the fairest and tenderest poetry of the Greeks is inspired by the rite. Here Sappho, with her epithalamia and hymeneal songs, shines supreme among the poets of the world. If, on the other hand, we should put all our faith in the comic poets of Athens, to whom women and marriage were always objects of satire, we should make the mistake of concluding that marriage was always in disfavor among young men. It is true that they generally waited until they were thirty or older before they settled down. But this, if we are to believe Plato, was as it should be. According to his theory of eugenics, harm was done by the mating of parents too young. Plato and Aristotle believed that the man should be between thirty and thirty-five years old, the girl should be from fourteen to twenty.

To perpetuate the state, to keep up the wor-

ship of the family gods and ancestors, and to
have sons and daughters who should care for
them in old age, were the frankly recognized
motives which led parents to arrange mar-
riages for their children. Such arrangement was
often made through the offices of a marriage-
agent. Certain positions in the government
were open only to married men, on the principle enunciated by Pericles: " a man's counsel
in a public crisis cannot have equal weight
when he has no children to risk in the common
danger." This is matched by the remark of
an American politician, that " no man will
shoulder a rifle to defend his boarding-house."

The Greek, in contrast to the Oriental, established the rule that no man should have
more than one wife. The agreement between
man and wife was a family, not a personal
affair. A formal contract was drawn and sub-
scribed to by the couple or their parents and
guardians, in the presence of witnesses. This
ceremony, really one of betrothal, not marriage,
was the only legal proceeding required. It provided for the sum of money, — for which goods
or real estate might be substituted, — which
the wife was to bring to her husband as
dowry, and for certain personal belongings

[58]

(*pherné*, later *parapherna*, *cf*. ' parapherna-
lia '), which she was to take as her own to her
husband's home. For all this property the
groom gave security to the bride's guardians,
engaging to return it in case of divorce. Men
preferred wives of their own social class, pos-
sessing wealth not too greatly in excess of their
own, and younger in years and experience. With
these conditions satisfied, it was felt that there
would be no awkward disparity, imperilling the
superiority of husband over wife. The law
of the Athenian commonwealth required that
citizens should marry only citizens, otherwise
their offspring were illegitimate so far as the
franchise was concerned. If, however, the relatives agreed to a match between citizen and
foreigner, their children were accounted legitimate in respect of the rights of inheritance, but
not of citizenship. Close relationship between
the married pair, barring only children of the
same mother, was no impediment. Often a male
relative was required to marry an heiress of his
family in order that her property might be retained under the family control.

The poor sacrificed their utmost to dower
their daughters well, in order to ensure for them
good treatment. So strong was this feeling, and

so great was the importance attached to the
dowry, that it has been transmitted in full
strength to the marriage customs of modern
Greece; and many a Greek is selling fruit or
flowers in America today for the chief purpose
of sending home money for his sister's dowry.
Few Greek men marry until they have thus
provided for their sisters' marriage. The poets
of old, like Sappho and Euripides, treat with
tender sympathy the lot of the young bride,
taken from her own associates to the house of
strangers. For the groom, if a young man, often
brought his wife to his father's house, to be
surrounded and controlled by his mother and
sisters. The mother-in-law joke, therefore, in so
far as it applies to the relations existing between a son-in-law and his wife's mother, is a
modern invention, since married men in Greece
did not live under the same roof with their
mothers-in-law. In antiquity it was the bride
and her husband's mother who came in close
contact, and possibly we should have had the
theme discussed earlier if women had expressed
themselves in literature. Euripides maintains
that they could; that they also knew the Muse;
but doubtless in many cases the forlorn little
bride found her mother-in-law no joke.

Yet, with all these disadvantages in her condition, the wife's property was well protected by the law. If the husband's goods were confiscated by the State in due process of law, her dowry could not be taken. Her children, not her husband, were her legal heirs. Her property was transferred under bond to her future husband at the betrothal, which was the essential part of the wedding.

On the wedding-day the bride's father offered sacrifice to Zeus, Hera, Artemis, and other marriage divinities. Water from the spring Calirrhoé was brought for the sacramental bath — an old custom to which the name Bridewell points — and votive offerings, a lock of hair, toys and dolls of her childhood, were dedicated to Artemis and the nymphs of the fountain. In the evening, when the moon was in the first quarter or full, the groom and his best man fetched his bride in a cart from her father's house. The Spartans required a husband to visit his bride at first in secret, a relic of marriage by theft once common. The 'best man' is perhaps the survivor of the custom today. In some parts of Greece in ancient times, and in Euboea today, the bridegroom comes suddenly, whence the saying: "Watch therefore,

for ye know not at what hour the bridegroom
cometh! " But the ceremony required no
priestly intervention, and the sacrifice offered
by the bride's father was the chief, if not the
only, religious ceremony connected with the
marriage. In the wedding procession songs
with flute or lyre accompaniment attended the
couple, whose dress, of course, was in festal
colors. The refrain, " Hymen, Hymenaeus O,"
and the torches carried by the mothers of the
couple, are often remembered in modern
poetry and symbolism.[5] This is true also of the
Epithalamium, sung by the company before
the closed door of the marriage chamber, and
first consecrated to literature by Sappho. Jokes
at the expense of the door-keeper or the married pair, and showering them with sweetmeats
or confetti, were as common then as now.

That the union thus contracted led to a
happy and loving life together is attested by
many cases. On the other hand widowhood
meant utter retirement and dependence, but,
since the woman was usually much younger
than her husband when he died, a second marriage for her was common.

7. BURIAL

THE mystery of life and death presents itself afresh, even to the primitive mind, whenever a birth, a marriage, or a funeral interrupts the regular course of family life. From the earliest times, therefore, religious ceremonies of an elaborate nature surrounded each of these occasions, and some of them are still maintained down to the present time in the practices of the folk. Religious conservatism is a potent force which weakens very slowly and gradually, so that the folklore and folk customs of people today still illustrate the traditional beliefs and customs of the Greeks in these matters. They will show many points of similarity with our own practices, although, in most cases, these have not been borrowed directly from theirs.

Curiously enough, the race does not seem to have detected early the sanitary motives which dictate the proper disposal of the bodies of the dead. Relatives and friends, of course, were reverently laid away, but in the earliest times, at least, it was allowable to bury them within the precincts of the house or near the market-place. The bodies of enemies, however, were mutilated and left to rot, and, even in

[63]

Plato's time, the noisome sight and smell of executed criminals cast into the pit outside the western walls of Athens often compelled the traveller to take another path. Yet again, very old legends reflect the growing belief that danger threatened a community if men killed in battle were not properly buried. The story of Antigone illustrates the growing fear, though it sprang from religious rather than sanitary causes. The spirit of the unburied body might rise to haunt and to harm the survivor. The danger to health which neglect of the dead brings to the living is first clearly apprehended by Thucydides, who graphically describes the awful contagion of the plague in 430 B.C. In Homer's time, a dead enemy, if his body had not been removed by his friends, was allowed to remain uncovered.

The civilization known as Mycenaean buried its dead; that described by Homer practiced cremation. In Athens, during the fifth and fourth centuries, both practices existed side by side, depending probably on the wishes of the dying, or the convenience of the survivors. In the Hellenistic Age, cremation seems to have been more common. The early Christians buried their dead.

Whatever the method, the utmost respect for what were called the 'customary rites' marked the details, and manifested the feeling of the survivors that the deceased was thenceforth an exalted spirit, who might return to haunt and molest the disrespectful and the negligent. Without these rites, too, the dead must wander in a kind of limbo which fringed the underworld, no longer a living being, nor yet accepted in the house of Hades — as though, like Hamlet's father, he had died " unhousel'd, disappointed, unaneled." And so, wherever the rites were duly observed, the dead lay in state for a whole day with a chaplet on the head, as token of its exalted power over the living, while friends brought ribbons and set jars of oil beside the couch. Elderly women, sometimes hired for the purpose, chanted ancient dirges, — a custom which is maintained in Greece today, and old women versed in the funeral chant are sometimes brought long distances to attend an Athenian funeral. The body was carried out, lying as in its last sickness on the same couch, covered only with a pall to keep the pollution of death from the sun-god. Songs of mourning, accompanied by the flute, were chanted as the procession of relatives and friends moved through the city and out of the gate to the ground where the body was to be buried or burned. In the latter case, it was laid upon a large pyre of logs, and when the last embers had been quenched by a libation of wine, the ashes were placed in an urn and interred.

The method of burying the unburned body varied in different places. At Athens, the necropolis occupied a beautiful region just outside the Dipylon, a great gate at the northwestern part of the wall. Here were erected tombs of marble or other stone. As late as the seventh century, the Athenians retained the custom, seen in Homer, of burying with the dead all kinds of household utensils, with gold diadems. Later, only the exquisitely wrought oil jars, known in our museums as Athenian white lekythoi, were deposited in the grave, and sometimes a piece of money was placed in the teeth for the needs of the last journey.

The form of the grave varied. On the islands and in Asia Minor, it was often hewn in the rock. But the ancient, even pre-Hellenic practice of rearing a mound over the remains persisted to a late period. It was then planted with ivy and flowers and covered with ribbons. Our

word ' tomb ' meant this kind of mound originally. Solon desired to check extravagance and
display at funerals and in burial, and about
his time — he was archon in 594 B.C. — it became customary to erect flat stones over the
graves. As time went on, these ' stelae ' received more and more adornment, and by the
middle of the fourth century they had entered
the domain of art in its most exquisite forms.
It became also the practice to lay a marble
pavement over the grave, and to place upon
it a large marble lekythos. The figure of a
siren, symbol of death, often surmounted the
top of a stelê. But the use of columns, so often
employed today, and of flat tables of stone
over the grave, still seen in old churchyards,
belongs to Hellenistic times. The broken columns of our modern cemeteries express a
sentiment which would have been foreign to
Greek modes of thought. Ornamented sar-
cophagi and large vaults in temple form belong
to the time of Alexander and later. The first
' mausoleum,' forty-six metres high, was
erected in Halicarnassus by Artemisia, widow
of the Persian satrap Maussollus, about the
middle of the fourth century B.C., and was accounted one of the seven wonders of the world.

Since death was regarded as a pollution, elaborate ceremonies were practiced to effect the purification of all who had been connected with the dead, and during the lying-in-state a jar of lustral water stood outside the front door so that all who went out of the house might sprinkle themselves before meeting their neighbors. If a man died in a temple or street, the whole district must be purified. No one who had touched a dead body might approach the gods. Hence in a Greek funeral, we note the entire absence of priestly ritual, of sacrifice to the gods, or of anything which resembles religious services for the dead. Christianity at least changed all this, and brought the mourners, through their dead, closer to the church and to the consolation which the church held out in the hope of resurrection. For the Greeks, it was necessary to purify the house where the dead had lain, as well as its inmates. There followed memorial banquets, in which the dead was regarded as the host, with libations and eulogies. Offerings were brought to the tomb on the ninth and the thirtieth day following the burial, and thereafter on the anniversary of the birth of the deceased. The custom of observing birthdays after the death of the person commemorated survives with us in the case of our national heroes. One of the days of the Anthesteria, a festival of Dionysus, was devoted to the dead; on this day spirits were supposed to return to earth. The Greek church today still celebrates its All Souls' Day in February, the month of the ancient Anthesteria, and offerings of grains are brought to the tomb exactly as in ancient times, except that the wheat is thought to symbolize the resurrection, following out St. Paul's illustration.

A special occasion was made of the memorial offerings for those who had fallen in battle. The great funeral oration of Pericles, pronounced over those who died in the first campaign of the Peloponnesian War, remains today as a model of restrained pride and reverence for the heroes of a nation.

8. The Physician

There was in ancient times, and perhaps is today, no profession grounded in, science which so touches the common daily life as that of the physician, and Americans may boast that the achievements of their surgeons, doctors, and dentists have helped greatly to restore the physician to the esteem and social position which he enjoyed among the Greeks, but which he lost, not wholly through his own fault, in Rome and in continental countries down to the nineteenth century. In Homer, the surgeon-physician is already an important economic unit, one of the recognized 'demiurgi,' or 'workers for the community.'

Medicine was established as a science — though the Greek called it an art — on the island of Cos, where the celebrated Hippocrates lived in the fifth century B.C. He was the first to record and to arrange his observations in a systematic whole; the first who tried to get behind symptoms to causes; the first to renounce any pretence of supernatural power. But even long before this, the Athenian Solon had written of the "soothing remedies" and the "gentle touch" of skilful physicians, while the poet Aeschylus speaks of the more drastic cutting and cauterizing to which they often had recourse. For a long time magic and religion were mixed with medical practice, and certain mistaken theories adversely affected the treatment of patients. For example, it was thought, down to a late period, that the veins were filled not with blood, but with breath;

and in the Middle Ages the Greek theory still persisted that the four humors, blood, phlegm, black bile, and yellow bile, determined a man's physical character as sanguine, phlegmatic, melancholic, or choleric, and that his health depended upon their proper mixture. Nevertheless, the numerous writings which have survived under the mighty name of Hippocrates reveal many sound principles, shrewd observations, and successful results to be credited to the devotion of him and his disciples. Surgeons were able to obtain both knowledge of the body and skill in operation in the casualties of war and the accidents of gymnastic exercise. The surgical instruments of a later day, found at Pompeii, reveal many likenesses to those in use now. What modern surgery and medicine could do without the use of Greek terms is a puzzle which fortunately requires no solution. *Anatomy, physiology, hygiene,* all the words in *-pathy, -iatry,* and *-therapy,* and countless names of diseases or pathological processes from *eczema* and *empyema* to *osteomyelitis* and *xerophthalmia,* readily proclaim themselves to be Greek; less easily recognized as Greek, because they were borrowed earlier, are *surgeon, cauterize, plaster,* and *practice.* The regimen which Greek physicians prescribed as safeguards against illness, their directions about diet, — a Greek word which signifies 'way of living' — baths, and bodily exercises remain as valid now as they were in old times. In Alexandria, in the third century, an institute of anatomy began the first scientific dissection leading to new and helpful discoveries, among which were the action of the heart, the confirmation of the fifth-century guess that the brain is the seat of consciousness, and the recognition, for the first time, of the nerves and their functions. Heretofore *neura* had meant only the sinews and ligaments. Passing from Alexandria to Rome, the Greek physician was in great demand during the Empire, and often exacted extraordinarily high fees. From that time until the sixteenth century Greek medicine was the norm of practice.

Physicians of the earlier time regarded themselves and their art as under the special tutelage of Asklepios (Aesculapius), god of healing, and often called themselves his sons, Asklepiadae. His symbol was the serpent, which was thought to be the type of rejuvenation, and is still to be seen in the insignia of medical officers of our army. On the south slope of the

Acropolis at Athens, and in the pleasant valley of Epidaurus in Argolis, were famous health-resorts consecrated to this god. Here the patients set up in gratitude for cures the tablets which recorded the nature of their disease and the cure which the god had prescribed through a dream, interpreted by his ministers. All this in time constituted a large and useful body of ' cases,' out of which grew the empirical knowledge of the Asclepiads.

The various sites in Greece consecrated to the god of healing and his attendant spirits — Hygieia, Panaceia — constitute the nearest ancient analogy to the modern hospital and sanitarium. Within the enclosure were temples, altars, walks, and grounds for exercise, and especially porticos, in which at night the patients lay and slept, hoping for the dream which, when interpreted by the priest in attendance, should indicate the procedure necessary to effect a cure. The act of lying on the ground, which thus became a ceremonial practice in the ancient regimen, may be traced back to the primitive view that direct contact with Mother Earth is in itself restorative; and whatever the sophisticated modern may think of this mingling of medicine with magic and religion, it is certain that the priests of Asklepios were able to amass a useful body of empirical knowledge which later grew to the proportions of a dignified science.

Although physicians were under no state control, and although there were undoubtedly quacks and charlatans among them, and Aristophanes called them all swindlers, they were, nevertheless, the first among professional men to establish an etiquette, an ethics, of their profession. Joined to the disadvantages under which they sometimes labored socially — Plato, for instance, classes them with artisans, intermarriage with whom no Athenian of the upper class would allow — they had much to overcome in the stupidity, ignorance, and distrust of many whom they sought to help. It was noticed with derision that the doctor could not treat himself. "Like a bad physician," says Aeschylus, "who cures others, but has no cure wherewith to heal himself;" a remark which recurs at the Crucifixion: "He saved others, himself he could not save." They were sometimes derided, also, for their pompous bearing, even for their fine clothes, but especially for their intricate apparatus, which, it was alleged, was designed merely to overawe the simple

[74]

layman. But in all this criticism it is easy to recognize the comic exaggeration of the professional joker, though no doubt some of their personal peculiarities were as well authenticated as those of any physician connected with a medical school today. The more forceful and individual he is, the more readily he lends himself to picturesque delineation. Galen, the great physician and medical writer of Roman times, tells of a bluff old doctor named Callianax (*ca.* 280 B.C.), who could no longer endure the fears and wails of a patient, and finally silenced him with the quotation " Even Patroclus died, and he was a better man than you." [6]

But the sober earnestness of the medical writings which have come down to us, the careful rules drawn up for the young physician, attest the high ideals which the profession set before itself. The ' Oath of Hippocrates ' is well-known today, and other injunctions have been traced back to him. On personal appearance he laid great stress. Hair, beard, and clothing must be so cared for as to leave only a pleasant impression on the patient. In bearing he should be calm, cheerful, guarded in what he says of the patient's condition. One provision of the Hippocratean oath points especially to fifth century conditions in Athens, though of course its terms are applicable to all periods: " I will maintain religiously the purity and integrity both of my conduct and of my art. Into whatever house I go, I will enter with the sole view of helping the sick, abstaining from all immodest acts toward women and slaves. If I hear anything that should not be revealed, I will regard it as a secret and observe religious silence on the subject." [7]

Still another requirement laid upon the young surgeon by the Roman Celsus points to the trying difficulties of operations without anaesthetics. According to him, the physician's sensibilities should be such that, resolved only on curing the patient submitted to his care, " he will not be moved by his cries of pain, he will not hurry more than circumstances require, or cut less than he must; but carry out everything as though he were not in the least affected by his patient's complaints."

Such is the story of one of the oldest professions. It begins with the revered Podaleirios and Machaon in the Homeric poems, veritable gods in the esteem of their helpless comrades;

it starts afresh with Hippocrates; it is honorably continued by many others, among whom was Nicomachus of Stageira, who as court physician in Macedonia at the end of the fifth century and beginning of the fourth may serve to illustrate both the scientific attainments and the social rank of its members later. The biological researches of his distinguished son Aristotle were probably largely inspired by the father. Surrounded by ignorance, burdened with the trappings of magic, which it took centuries to shake off, the ' art of the physician ' reveals the steady progress of the Greeks in what William James used to call the most humane of all studies.

III. IN THE SCHOOL

1. EDUCATION

OF ALL the races of antiquity, the Greeks were probably the most child-loving. This can be maintained in spite of the custom of exposing new-born babes, especially girls, which we read of in some periods of economic stress and among certain classes of the population. If the age in which we live is preëminently the age of the child, the tendency already finds its spring in the fifth century interest in children, their education, and their part in the life of family and of state. It was the ambition of normal Athenian parents to have capable, devoted children to provide for their old age and to perpetuate the worship of the family ancestors.

In Sparta, a commission of old men inspected a new-born child and determined whether its physical condition warranted the preservation of its life for the military needs of the state. The fallacy of such measures taken in the name of efficiency is easily proved by the history of

many men and women who in spite of poor
health and weak bodies have guided the
thought and action of their fellows. In Athens,
the father had the right to acknowledge the
child as his own or to decree that it should be
exposed. If he recognized it, according to regular forms of a ceremony held five days after
birth, he was bound by law and custom to
protect and rear it, and he never had the
autocratic power of life and death which
theoretically belonged to the Roman *patria
potestas*.

Ten days after birth a name was bestowed
with proper formality. Names always bore an
intelligible meaning and were of good omen.
Their etymological significance could be recognized, in almost all cases, as soon as the name
was pronounced. Thus Pericles is ' he of ex-
ceeding glory;' Sophocles, ' of glorious wisdom.' Of course this intelligibility was once an
obvious attribute of modern ' Christian ' names
bestowed on children, though time has dimmed
the original meanings of Teutonic names like
Alfred and William, and Greek names like
George and Margaret. Robert, for example,
means the same as the Greek Lamprocles, ' of
illustrious fame.' The meaning of our surnames

is understood, now, only by the philologist and
the genealogist. But with the Greeks the meaning of proper names was still consciously felt,
and the naïve method of naming the child by
one of these descriptive appellatives indicated
the simpler social and political organization of
the Athenians and Spartans, as contrasted with
that of the Romans, whose system of naming
was as elaborate as that of the most highly
civilized states today. " What's in a name? "
A great deal, as may be seen by reading Booker
Washington's account of how he acquired his,
and what it meant to him as an emblem of
civic importance. And so the ' name-day ' was
one to be cherished in the after-life of the
child when grown to manhood, as it is in many
countries of Europe today, since it was the day
which gave the child his civic status.

The name of an Athenian child, as registered
by the father in the records of his brotherhood
and deme, would read, for example, " Socrates,
son of Sophroniscus, of the deme Alopekê
(Foxborough)." There were no family names
in this early society, although it was sometimes
the practice to give boys of the same family
names compounded of similar elements, such
as Demosthenes, Demomeles, and Demotimus,

all kinsmen. The oldest male child commonly received the name of his paternal grandfather.

The devoted interest bestowed by Greeks upon all sorts of toys and games roused the wonder and derision of the sober Romans. There is scarcely a toy given to children today which had not its prototype in the Greek nursery. The rattle, the ball, the doll, both stiff-legged and jointed, the cart, toy dishes, jackstones, hoops, are a few of the more common. Children also kept pets of many kinds, beginning, of course, with the dog. But the cat, which is a latecomer into European family life, was missing from the fireside in classical times; instead, the literature and the monuments tell of monkeys and fawns, tortoises and weasels, quails, pigeons, and jackdaws as not infrequent members of the household.

The Greek child's games are still played in the streets and vacant lots of our towns today: hide-and-seek, ducks and drakes, duck-on-a-rock, blind man's buff (of which there were three varieties), tug-of-war, and ball. For many of these games, especially those played by the younger children, appropriate verses were sung in accompaniment.

The education of an Athenian child was

wholly dependent on the father. The State had no part in it. Plato and Aristotle protested against the individualism of Athenian education and other institutions, but their protests came at the close of the great period of Athenian life, and so could have little effect until much later times. In the richer families an old slave was assigned to attend the boy wherever he went until he was sixteen. He taught the boy proper deportment in the street and elsewhere, took him to school and brought him home. The relation between the two, or at least the feeling of the boy towards his school, may be inferred from the proverb, " as sour-faced as boys going to school." Private teachers in charge of small schools taught the separate branches, grammatiké, music, and gymnastics. The first included the elements of reading and writing, Homer, Hesiod, and other old writers being the texts from which the teachers gathered their material. Another favorite text was the *Beast Fables* of Aesop, charged with the simple, practical wisdom of many centuries of human experience. A modern writer on education has contended that these Fables, originating in the East and presumably inculcating blind obedience to Asiatic

despotism, are unfit for the boy or girl of democratic America, and to prove his theory he
cites the well-known story of the oak, which
resisted the storm and was carried away, while
the yielding reed rose up again unharmed.
Unluckily for his contention, this very fable
is chosen by Sophocles to warn a tyrant against
proceeding too far against the popular will —
a proof, if any were needed, that the Greek boy
extracted his own moral from these sources,
and left the evil unnoticed, if evil there was.

The boy learned his letters, then combined
them into syllables, then into words and sentences, learning inflections by using the same
word in different syntactical combinations. In-
cidentally, though he had no text books, perhaps because of it, he stored his memory with
the lines of the great poets, and imbibed knowledge of the history and aspirations of his race,
of warfare and citizens' duties, of geography
and such other matters as these poets touched
upon in their verse. It will readily be seen that
the object of education was not the accumu-
lation of facts so much as the training and
discipline of character. " Reverence and obedience," says Goethe, " should be the aim of the
teacher," and the Greeks sought these qualities

above all others. In a letter, one of the oldest now extant, the philosopher Epicurus writes thus to a little boy of whose upbringing he had taken charge: " It is good if you also are in health and obey your grandfather and uncle in all things, as you have done before. For be sure, the reason why I and all the others love you so much is that you obey them in all things." [8]

In writing, the boy followed the master's dictation, using small tablets of boxwood, the surface of which was covered over with wax, hardened by the admixture of gypsum or tar, and protected from rubbing by raised edges, like those of a slate. Two or three slates of this sort were strung together by a cord, to form a ' diptych' or ' triptych.' The boy incised the letters with a sharp pointed bronze graver, ' graphis,' the top of which swelled to a wide surface useful for erasing. As he grew more expert, he was allowed the use of ink, made of lamp black, and applied by a quill to a papyrus scroll. Papyrus was imported from Egypt, where it grew in the form of a tall cane by the river Nile. The pith or marrow of the stalk was extracted from the stem of the plant, rolled into thin sheets, two of which were pressed transversely, *i.e.*, with fibres crosswise, against each other to make the finished writing material. Since it was expensive, authors usually wrote the rough drafts of their works on tablets, transcribing them later to papyrus rolls (*biblia*). Later, animal skins of goats, sheep, and calves were perfected as writing material in Pergamum, whence comes the word 'parchment.' Paper (from 'papyrus'), 'Bible' (collection of books), 'bibliography' and 'tome' are some of the familiar words which our language has taken over from the book-craft of Greece. Public bulletins, laws, and proclamations were scratched in wax or gypsum spread on wooden boards; more permanent inscriptions were incised on bronze or marble; and for meaner purposes, such as tax-receipts, voting on a citizen's status, and the like, the people even wrote on pieces of broken pottery, (*ostraka*, *cf.* 'ostracism'). We may safely assume that most male citizens in Athens knew the art of writing in the fifth century. Women learned it only occasionally before the Hellenistic Age.

Only the elements of numbers and counting were taught in the schools, and most Greeks liked to count on the fingers. The decimal system prevailed accordingly, but there are also many traces of the duodecimal and sexagesimal modes of counting, which have survived in such collectives as dozen and score (one-third of sixty) and in the number of hours in the day, minutes in the hour, and degrees in the circle.

In Sparta, the state undertook the care of the boy after his seventh year, but interested itself in his bodily development more than in the cultivation of the finer intellectual qualities. Trickery and evasion were even encouraged, since body and mind were to be later devoted to the strenuous exertions and deceptive practices of war. Gymnastics and even music were pursued solely with reference to their military value and uses. Exercises tending to strengthen the muscles rather than athletic sports which include the element of fun were prescribed in the Spartan system. Choral music and choral singing, which served for marching and battle, not solo singing in which individual talent might be displayed, were thought to serve more suitably the requirements of their socialistic régime. As in all aristocratic communities, the moral qualities desired included

reverence for one's elders and superiors, obedience to the state, uncomplaining endurance of
danger and pain, and strict reserve in conduct
and conversation.

By the fifth century Greek literature had
developed three great forms of poetry, epic,
dramatic, and lyric. Lyric poetry comprised the
choral song, the special contribution of the
Dorians, and the solo or individual song,
written for every conceivable occasion of worship or private life, and expressing every mood
and aspiration of the human heart. Many of
these the boy had learned at his mother's knee,
but they were so various that no generic term
to denote them all was known in the classical
period. The word ' lyric,' from ' lyre,' appears
very late, not much before the time of Cicero,
but it correctly suggests the close connection
of this kind of poetry, as distinguished from
epic or dramatic, with the harp or lyre. Playing the lyre, therefore, formed an essential
part of the school curriculum, quite necessary
in the eyes of a music-loving and singing
people. The number of musical instruments
known to them was few, but they embraced
the three types represented today in any
orchestra: string, wind, and percussion instru-

ments. The last, such as the tambourine, cymbals, glockenspiel, and castanets, were regarded with some disfavor. They were not native instruments, but had come in from the Orient, and suggested the wilder, orgiastic practices of Eastern religions. The three wind instruments in ordinary use were the Pan's pipe, a series of seven (later nine) graduated pipes bound together by withes and wax; the *auloi* or double pipes, each having a reed in the mouthpiece at the end, like a clarinet; and the trumpet, used in battle, in ritual, and on all occasions where signals were to be given in large gatherings of the people. For a short period during the early fifth century, the boy received instruction in the pipes or flute; but the playing of the flute precluded singing by the player, and so it passed to the professional musician, who accompanied with it the choruses' in the theatre, the conduct of athletic events at the games, and the marching of troops. There remained, therefore, the lyre, which consisted of a sounding box, originally a tortoise shell, into which were inserted two horns with a connecting cross bar, from which the strings (four or seven) were stretched to the sounding box. Held in the left hand, the player with his right struck the notes with the plectrum, a metal striker or key, modulating or silencing the strings with the fingers of his left hand. This slight instrument is the precursor of the guitar, the mandolin, the zither, the violin and all its family, the modern harp, and the pianoforte, all of which show a constant increase in resonant power and tonal variety. The pipes, for their part, were the first instruments to be developed by virtuosi, in the latter part of the fifth century, and their requirements led first to the invention of the cross flute (the ordinary flute of today), the organ (*organon,* or ' instrument ' *par excellence*), grandest of them all, and the host of wood and brass instruments, down to the saxophone, which are played in every band today.

That music has lasting moral effects the Greeks were profoundly convinced, and there seems to have been a controversy against the innovations in rhythm and in harmony which lasted from Aristophanes' time to Plato's, and which our censors have revived today in their descriptions of the effect of jazz and other orgiastic music. Plato would banish from his state the " soft Lydian airs " of Ionia and the East, as being too sensuous and enervating,

[89]

retaining the Dorian mode for its strongly martial character, and the grave and plaintive Phrygian. Indeed Plato, like a good many reformers from his time to Tolstoy and later, was strong for a censorship both in music and in literature.

While the Spartans practiced bodily training for military ends, the Athenians indulged their more genial and sprightly nature by combining the elements of exercise and sport. They planned their gymnastic training ever with the conscious aim of producing not only a sound mind in a sound body, but also a beautifully organized body to match a harmonious, well-balanced spirit and soul. Hence the exercises prescribed for the boy in the *palaestra* (wrestling school) stopped short of the more rigorous and sometimes brutal boxing matches and the *pankration,* a combination of wrestling and boxing. The Athenians professed disgust for the broken-nosed, split-eared, and cracked-fingered boxer, who to their minds was a gluttonous beef-eater when not in training, and a sordid pot-hunter when he was. On the contrary, in the palaestra the boy learned how to run, jump, wrestle, throw the discus, and cast the spear, and few there were who did not know how to swim and dive. Of a dunce, it was said: " He can neither swim nor spell." But the aim always was to develop a supple, symmetrical body, and above all a spirit of courage and of generous rivalry, the power to measure and cope with the resources of an adversary, and at the same time to use only the method of fair play. This was Aristotle's ideal, and there can be no doubt that the Athenians, in their great period, realized it to an extraordinary degree. A gymnasium was a public grove or park, with pleasant walks and open spaces suitable for exercises. Such was the famous Academy where Plato taught, and the Lyceum, in which Aristotle had his school. Hither, therefore, the philosophers came, sure of having young men for an audience, or older men who had gathered to watch the training of some famous athlete. Not until the Hellenistic age does the gymnasium become a formal building, with running track, wrestling grounds, dressing rooms, and baths.

The words academy and lyceum have passed into familiar and honorable use in most modern languages. In their present meaning they reveal the new direction which education took with the coming of the Sophists, the first professors of higher learning. Their age is called the age of enlightenment, for in it the Greeks, and especially the Athenians, turned their studies toward the capacities and limitations of the human mind, and evolved theories of the universe, of personal conduct, of religion and life, very different from the more naïve conceptions which had prevailed in the earlier times. With it came a tendency, seen in some European countries today, to regard bodily training as of secondary importance in education, and another tendency, whose devastating effects may be seen chiefly in America, to relegate athletics to a special class of experts whose feats are watched and applauded by an idle crowd of onlookers. Aristophanes complains of this fault in the last years of the fifth century. Professional training became the goal in all branches, and education passed from its function of training the boy, by culture of mind and body, for his duties as a member of society, to the development of special methods, which we call vocational, invented to train him for some work or profession.

In this spirit and with this intent the Sophists carried their own learning and teaching laudably beyond the narrow limits of the teacher

of reading and writing, though these funda-
mentals were always assumed in the young men
who resorted to them. The new teachers wrote
treatises on formal grammar, on the use of
words and construction of sentences and above
all, on the art of public speaking. Less laud-
able was their object to secure immediate re-
turns for their pupils in successful debate, in
swaying crowds, in winning lawsuits. Matter
was sacrificed to form, and honesty often gave
way to sharp practice. The evil connotation of
the words sophistry and sophistication remains
to damn their activity in the minds of men
from their time to ours. And yet without the
Sophists we should hardly have had Plato and
Aristotle, their determined opponents; and
without Plato and Aristotle it is impossible to
conceive of modern philosophy and science.

The Sophists, too, may be credited with the
spread of the professional ideal in other lines.
Some of them introduced higher mathematics,
geometry plane and solid, and astronomy; also
the theory of music. They are responsible for
the idea of technique, or professional skill and
technical knowledge as opposed to dilettant-
ism and the aims of the amateur. Through
their inspiration, which affected all branches

of activity, arose the conception of war as something to be carried on by trained soldiers, as an art involving tactics and strategy as well as the more skilful use of sword and spear by individuals. In the fifth century every able-bodied citizen expected to bear his part when danger threatened the nation. In the fourth century Plato assumes that the day of " the embattled farmer " has passed, and that only a strict training can prepare the soldier, especially assigned for the purpose, to resist an enemy.

This is only one example of the growth of specialization and professionalism in the fourth century, consequent upon the teaching of the Sophists in the fifth. They were preparing men's minds for larger enterprises in science, politics, and ethics. They had, without knowing it, heralded a time when the narrow limits of the little city-state, fervid and patriotic though it was, were to be transcended by wider conceptions which culminated in the empire-state, and made easy the transition to the concept of man as member of a great human brotherhood. In the city-state, with the small but ever-present contacts of all classes, there could be no sharp distinction drawn between government and society. Henceforth, however, we have the germs of a separate economics, a separate politics, a separate ethics, though they are still treated as one by Aristotle.

Coinciding with this movement we can detect a change in religion which was to lead in Hellenistic times either to a complete breakdown of the older systems, or a hard and sterile eclecticism which dared not deny altogether, but which afforded little inspiration to the springs of conduct. What religion the boy learned in the fifth century was very real and potent in his adult life. He imbibed it in the stories of gods and goddesses told by his nurse or mother. He enlarged his knowledge in the school-study of Homer, Hesiod, Theognis, and the other poets. Sacrifices at home conducted by his father, or at the temples on the occasion of state festivals by the priests, taught him more of ritual, worship, and legend. But his moral training largely depended upon other influences, in the home, in contact with his elders and other boys, and upon the lessons of conduct to be drawn from the poets. It was left for the Sophists, and above all for Socrates, who, though not a Sophist, shared in their spirit of enquiry, to begin a system of ethics which

Plato expanded and Aristotle elaborated into more or less formal precepts.

2. THE SCIENCES

To TREAT adequately of all the arts and sciences which occupied the labors of Greeks, whether in the sphere of the industries, practical arts, or in the field of pure science, would require a discussion of many technological facts which are outside our present scope: it would, in fact, amount to a history of science, beginning with its origins and later affected by the new impulses given to knowledge by the Sophists. However much this early science may be disregarded by historians who have eyes only for the achievements of men since the revival of learning, we have to remember that the Renaissance itself was the re-discovery of Greek and Roman inspiration, and that without the vocabulary which the Greek and the Latin bequeathed, modern terminologies would be helpless. Merely Teutonic or Celtic material could never have supplied terms so convenient as *electron, ion, cathode,* to say nothing of *telegraph, telephone,* and *radio.*

One of the oldest sciences, astronomy, derives the names of the constellations, the planets in the solar system, and many terms like ' apogee ' from Greek usage. Even the Arabic names of stars, such as Betelgeuse, are a reminder that the Arabs studied astronomy through the inspiration of the Greeks. Not only could eclipses be predicted by men like Thales in the sixth century before the Christian era; the ordinary mariner or wayfarer by land laid his course or traced his path by his knowledge of the stars. Attempts to show that Euripides could make a mistake about the rising of Sirius have failed, and it is doubtful if any Greek, living as he did on more familiar terms with nature than we do today, could have blundered as a recent novelist does when she pictures the crescent moon as setting, only to reappear a few pages later and light the path of the hero when he confronts the villain.

The professional sciences had their root and origin in the speculation of Ionian philosophers from Thales onward. Gradually, they emerged, on the one hand, from philosophy, and on the other, from the simple practical data of common experience shared by the ordinary man. Aristotle laid the foundations in the fourth century, when, building upon the solid ground of Socratic induction, he established through

observation and possibly experiment a system
of classification which is fundamental to all
exact knowledge. But even before him, Anaxagoras and Democritus, especially the latter,
had introduced in the fifth century an atomic
conception of matter which, reformed and expanded, is the basis of chemistry and physics
today. That the earth was a globe was maintained by the oldest Pythagoreans, who conceived that it and the planets (including the
sun) revolved round a mighty central fire. The
revolution of the earth on its axis was recognized by Ecphantus, and in the third century
Aristarchus of Samos proposed a heliocentric
conception of the universe — an idea, to be
sure, which was not finally adopted until many
centuries afterwards, when it was revived by
Copernicus (1543 A.D.).

Geographical knowledge expanded rapidly
from the first ventures of Ionian sailors into
unknown seas (p. 106), so that even in Aeschylus' time the rich variety of household stores
imported into Athens is a matter of comment.
Geographical description formed at first a part
of history, and indeed down to a late time
was called ' historia,' when it was finally sepa-
rated by Eratosthenes, head of the Alexandrian

library, and became a special study. At that time the Greeks had long since outgrown the Homeric conception of a small flat world surrounded by a river (Oceanus) and containing a sea in the middle ('Mediterranean'); and the known world (*oikoumené, cf.* 'ecumenical') now stretched from the Ganges westward beyond the Pillars of Heracles (Gibraltar) and on to the coast of Britain and the shores of the Baltic. Eratosthenes constructed a map with longitude and latitude indicated, having noticed that in Alexandria, at the time of the summer solstice, the sun was 7 1/6° from the zenith, while at Syene (Assouan) it entirely illuminated a deep well, *i.e.* it was directly overhead.

In mathematics,[9] it goes without saying, the ordinary Greek of the fifth century had not progressed beyond the elements of arithmetic learned in his youngest boyhood and retained in the commoner processes of business. Yet this same century, so fruitful in other achievements, saw a great advance in mathematics made chiefly by the Pythagoreans. They demonstrated some of the most important principles of plane and solid geometry as well as arithmetical and geometrical proportion. It is owing to their method of proof, which involved not formulas, but lines and surfaces, that we of today speak of the ' square ' or the ' cube ' of a number, of ' powers ' and ' roots,' — conceptions which properly belong to geometry, and were later carried over into arithmetic and algebra. The third century witnessed, at Alexandria, the culmination of mathematical accomplishment in Euclid, who built up a logical system of arithmetic and geometry which has formed the basis of mathematics ever since. Meanwhile the celebrated Archimedes of Syracuse had laid the foundations of mechanics and engineering, largely through the development of siege engines in the century preceding. To him also we owe the discovery of specific gravity, the invention of the screw, the windlass, and the lever. " Give me a place to stand," he said, " and I will move the earth." The ' artillery ' which he devised for the defense of Syracuse remained essentially the same until the introduction of explosive powder.

And so the great movement begun by the Sophists, in spite of mistakes and failings natural to all beginnings, culminated in the Hellenistic period in what may be correctly described as the idea of a university, in the sense that all fields of human knowledge then attainable were 'professed' by specially trained men, who 'announced' subjects for lectures and discussions, and became 'professors,' a Latin translation of the Greek word used in this connection to mean 'announce' or 'advertise.' Seated on high thrones above the level of their hearers, who numbered both students and educated persons in society, they maintained, doubtless, the aloofness, the air of authority, the dignified bearing, that are supposed to belong to university professors. But like the modern professor, they were often the butt of popular ridicule, and concerning one of these ancient 'Dry-as-dusts' we have a mock epigram which recites that he had just seven pupils — the four walls and three empty benches.[10]

There were pedantry and dullness, but there was brilliancy too. For even though Alexandria had become, through the generous patronage of the Ptolemies, the centre of literature, art, and science, Athens was not entirely superseded and forgotten, and no visitor there could fail to be reminded of the past glories of the city, or fail to note the lasting versatility, the mental alertness, the redeeming humor of her people.

Down to the closing of the pagan schools by
Justinian, Athens remained the seat of instruction in philosophy to which young Romans
like Cicero and Horace resorted as a matter
of course. Further, the lavish endowments of
prizes became common, and rich citizens provided gymnasia with elaborate furnishings and
equipment, which included, besides the special
arrangements for exercises, covered exedrae,
and porticos where philosophers taught, reci-
tations of tragedies, comedies, and mimes were
given, musical contests held — all in delightful
surroundings embellished by painting and
sculpture. In architecture, the temple, which
had been supreme in the classical period, is
now rivalled by the gymnasium. Programmes
of studies, with lists of educational commis-
sioners and other state officials, who, like the
gymnasiarch, were appointed to oversee the
conduct and the work of the students, were
published and posted, reminding one of the
school and college catalogues of our own time.
Add to this other documents in stone which
have come down to us from the ruins: class
lists, with indication of the rooms to which
classes were assigned; awards of prizes; lists
of clubs; notices of holidays, memorial days,

gymnastic events, and even final examinations; and the modern reader wonders whether he has not been transported suddenly from the second century to the twentieth. It was in this period that Hadrian, imperial patron of the new Athens, founded the Athenaeum, an institution whose associations with our higher education today place it almost in the rank of Academy and Lyceum.

And the girls? We have seen that a kind of education existed in Sparta, so far as gymnastic training was concerned. This was utterly repugnant to Athenian taste and practice. Yet even in Athens, girls occasionally learned at home to read and write, though their knowledge was casual and their chances of obtaining it were uncertain. But they learned to sing and dance, sometimes to play the lyre, and their opportunities increased in Plato's time. Even Euripides knows the blue-stocking and the female *savante,* though possibly his conception may have been derived from the Ionian Aspasia rather than from any woman of Athens. His Phaedra knew how to write, his Iphigenia did not. No female poet rose to prominence in Athens. In the art of weaving and embroidering, however, the Athenian girls were proficient, and if they were restrained and inhibited from other modes of self-expression, they are amply avenged today, for embroidery by women is the one native art of any consequence that survives in Greece.

IV. IN THE MARKET–PLACE

1. COMMERCE AND INDUSTRIES

WHEN we try to picture the daily life of the Greeks outside the home, we must avoid the mistake of confusing the habits of different classes of the people. The notion that all Greeks spent the morning in idle conversation in the market-place, or sitting as jurors in the law-courts, or exercising in the gymnasia, is not tenable. It is true that Pericles cherished the hope that all adults of the citizen class might have leisure to give themselves wholly to political affairs; and he could realize this hope partially by instituting pay for jurors. At a later date pay was given for attendance even at the popular assembly. Nevertheless, many Athenians of the richer sort, who could well afford to sit on juries without pay, renounced the 'leisure' which was the ideal of philosopher and statesman, and were active in wholesale trade; many were engaged in wars, either waged by their own country or by other countries to which they proffered their services; and outside the city, of course, large numbers of farmers, herdsmen, sailors, and others were more or less continually at work. This work slackened during the winter, and at no time, seemingly, was it as rigidly exacting as the work required by modern industrial methods, except in the case of persons in great poverty, like the weaver in Aristophanes or the fishermen in one of the Theocritean idyls.

The versatility of the Greek genius made them the one people in history who have acquired distinction in trade and in sport as well as in the great things of the mind. In contrast with the Romans, their tolerant attitude toward business and their talent for commerce and industry are among their most characteristic racial features. Of course, this does not apply to the rigid, aristocratic Spartan of the upper class, nor does it exclude, even in the mind of the Athenian, a certain contempt for the peddler, the retail-dealer, and the petty tradesman in the small necessities of life. Nor were money-lenders in high repute, at least before the fourth century.

Far back in the eighth century the Ionian seaman began to push his barque into the

waters where, in Homeric times and later, the
Phoenicians had sailed and traded with no
competitors.[11] From Euboea the men of Chalcis, accomplished iron-workers, established
settlements on the coast of Macedonia and
Thrace. The island of Thasos, bleak though it
seemed to the men of the south, lured them
with its gold. The strategic and commercial importance of the Dardanelles (Hellespont) was
early recognized by the Milesians, who, with
men of the other cities as well, planted nearly
a hundred colonies along the shores which the
Great War has introduced to the knowledge
of Americans — Gallipoli (the Thracian Cher-
sonesus), the Sea of Marmora (Propontis) —
and farther out into the dangerous, inhospitable
Black Sea, both on the northern and southern
side, or what is now Russia, Armenia, and
Turkey. For the broad spaces of Pontus and
the Russian steppes — then Scythia — furnished abundant cargoes of wheat; and in the
north the Greeks learned of other dairy products besides their own cheese of goat's or
sheep's milk, especially the curious golden
butter (a Greek word), which Thracians knew
how to get from the milk of cows. From the
Greek mainland, also, colonists sailed to found

Byzantium (Constantinople, Stamboul) and Chalcedon, two cities destined to play a great part in the culture of Europe. Milesian adventurers also penetrated into Egypt, and left there one of the oldest examples of Greek hand-writing, some names of soldiers in the pay of King Psammetichus, idly scrawled on the leg of a colossal statue.[12] Two English words survive to attest the humor of these doughboys in a foreign land, — ' crocodile,' which really means a small lizard, and ' ostrich,' which originally meant a sparrow.[13] On the north African coast, Greeks from Thera colonized Cyrene, whence came an herb, silphium, which seasoned Greek dishes wherever Greek cooks were to be found. In the west the great cities of Syracuse, Agrigentum, Tarentum, Sybaris, — home of the luxurious Sybarites — Naples, and Marseilles arose to transmit Greek civilization to a savage or barbarous Europe. And so the Semitic culture of the Phoenicians, such as it was, gave way to the better influences of the Greek, who thus established himself as the spiritual ancestor of all the West. Semitic Carthage survived the longest, to be finally destroyed by Rome.

In Greece itself the lines of trade began

and ended in cities like Corinth, Chalcis and
Eretria in Euboea, in the island of Aegina, and
in Athens (Peiraeus); and many provisions of
modern admiralty laws and customs are rooted
in the nautical experience of this early time.
Liability for loss or damage by storm and ship-
wreck was adjudicated by regular process and
trade customs. Marine insurance today inherits
still something of the Greek procedure in case
of loss by fire or jettison. Sparta took no part
in this maritime activity except in the founding
of Tarentum; within her own limits, trade was
rigorously banned for the aristocratic and conservative Spartiates. Only the Perioeci, who
had no political rights, might engage in trade
and industry, but their use of iron money naturally precluded foreign commerce. Thebes, another agricultural state, allowed no part in the
government to men who had been in trade
within ten years of their candidacy for office.

The earliest financial legislation of which we
get clear reports was instituted by Solon, who
so reformed the currency of Athens as to bring
it into relation with the gold coinage of her
neighbor and commercial rival Euboea. Heretofore, the silver system of Aegina had prevailed,
and we may detect in his reform the rudiments

of the gold standard which prevails, or before
the Great War prevailed, in most commercial
states today. In commerce Athens slowly won
a supremacy which she retained until the age of
the Ptolemies, when she retired before the competition of Corinth and especially of Rhodes
and Alexandria. When Corinth was destroyed
in 146 B.C., Athens enjoyed a brief revival until
her own downfall at the hands of Sulla in
86 B.C. Thereafter there came only an artificial
restoration in the time of Hadrian, to be followed by many centuries of obscurity until, a
hundred years ago, Greece struggled out of
the domination of the Turk, and the port of
Peiraeus once more began to fill with ships
from all over the world.

The foreign and wholesale trade of Athens
was conducted largely by her own citizens,
now and then by a few Egyptians, Syrians, and
other foreigners; retail trade, which old-fashioned Athenians despised, was in the hands of
the metics (or resident aliens) and poorer citizens. Aristophanes provides pictures of the
shrewd sausage seller — ' hot dog ' vendor —
peddling his meats in the street, and of the
poor little old woman hurrying to market to
sell her embroidery, — both of them ignorant

and poverty-stricken, but of the citizen class. It is a mistake to assume that a large proportion of the cheaper trade and industry of Athens was carried on by slaves alone.

The thin soil of Greece, especially of Attica, made it necessary to import grain from Egypt, Sicily, and south Russia, exactly as in modern times. Other imports were gold from Thrace, timber from Macedonia, papyrus writing material from Egypt, rugs from Persia; and after Alexander's conquests had opened the East to Greek caravans, spices, metals, and precious stones came in more abundantly. Exports were wool and woolen garments, olive oil, and wine; also from Athens, in the great days when her artisans were artists, went out cargoes of rich and varied earthenware and metal vessels, arms and armor, bronze statues and other works of art, furniture of wood and of bronze, besides the humbler casks of olives, figs, and fish in oil or pickle.

Farming in Greece has always been difficult, except in the plain of Thessaly or the low, moist lands of Boeotia, and one or two narrow strips of fertile country of Peloponnesus. The Greeks themselves remarked the traditional conservatism of the farmer, — his proneness to adhere to the ways of his fathers. In Greece today, although the Ames plow has made its way into the country, the traveller may also see the plowman turning over a shallow furrow with the same primitive plow which Hesiod prescribed seven centuries before the Christian era. But the poor soil and dry climate in most regions exacted and produced considerable skill in irrigation, and from earliest times the land has been cut with tiny rivulets of water carefully drawn from springs and rivers.

In Asia Minor, land of wide empires, agriculture was practiced on vast estates, the centres of which became large and important cities. In Greece, on the contrary, the farmer lived on a small isolated holding, as in Colonial America, or, as in Continental Europe today, in villages, going some distance to and fro to work in the fields during the season. In very remote districts, the picture of the " self-sufficing " estate which we have in the *Odyssey* and in Hesiod's *Works and Days,* remains true even in the classical period. Here the master joined actively in the manual labor of his dependents. Odysseus knew how to build a house, forge his tools, make a boat, and cook his dinner. In

Lacedaemon, however, where the true Spartiates scorned manual work, agriculture was carried on by the subordinate Perioeci and the serfs called Helots. In the fourth century the absentee landlord begins to raise problems even in Attica, where an overseer, who might be a slave himself, often had charge of the estate. But this is also the period of the gentleman farmer, like Xenophon and Ischomachus. Three plays of Aristophanes, the *Acharnians,* the *Clouds,* and the *Peace,* give us the best picture of the small farmer and the simple virtues which were ascribed to him.

Into Athens, also, flowed the coins from many mints; exchange and banking thrived, and many modern usages in finance were instituted. Money was loaned up to fifty or sixty per cent of the value of property pledged as security. The principle that every bargain is at the purchaser's risk prevailed against Plato's protest. Bargains were concluded only by haggling or competitive bidding, since goods were not offered at fixed prices; the latter method is a very late and, on the whole, American practice. Goods were paid for in cash, or, if credit was extended, payment was expected at the end of the month. Bills of exchange, letters of credit, and checks were unknown, but promissory notes were accepted though apparently not negotiable. The oral promise, if made in the presence of a witness, was usually accounted more binding. The word ' bank ' — *i.e.*, bench — recalls the Greek origin of banks and banking, since the bench corresponds to the table on which the money-changers piled their coins. Coinage was maintained by such states as Athens, Corinth, and Syracuse at a high level of purity; some debasing is noted in Athens in the troubled times near the close of the Peloponnesian War, but not on any such ruinous scale as has been witnessed in Russia and Germany today. Paper money, and fiat money in general, was unknown.

The currency was based on a system of weights which was ultimately derived from Babylonia, and which probably lies at the basis of all systems in use today except, of course, the metric. It was in use many generations before the rich and powerful Lydians of the seventh century B.C. invented coined money. Before that time the weights were used in barter and exchange, scales being necessary for every transaction. Otherwise value was expressed in terms of cattle. A girl in Homer's time was said to be worth so many cows, just as a girl in a North American Indian tribe brought her father so many ponies, the price her suitor must pay for her in marriage. One cow was worth ten sheep, and gradually other commodities became exchangeable with the cow as the standard or unit of value. Such commodities were vessels of silver, gold, bronze, and iron, metals in the form of arms and armor, metals in lumps or bullets (bullion), and slaves. When, finally, pieces of metal came to have more or less fixed weights attached to them, and bore a stamp, thus becoming coins, we find that coins bear a definite relation to the system of weights which preceded them. What was originally a ' pound ' (*mnâ*) in weight, came to be thought of as a pound of gold or of silver specifically, though there was no coin of that amount. The Athenians never lost consciousness of this intimate relation between their money and their weights, and to this day it is customary in some Greek banks when handling large sums of gold to weigh rather than count them.

The establishment of a fixed standard takes a long time, and is brought about only after much commercial intercourse among fairly civilized nations. The early Dutch traders on Manhattan Island, according to the mocking narrative of Washington Irving, used to weigh the skins brought to them by the Indians and placed in one scale-pan, against the fists of the traders placed in the other. " The rule of thumb " survives to prove that the earliest Greeks adopted this rough and ready method of measuring lines. Similarly, in the gradual transfer of Eastern weights to the Western world, the unit known as the talent varied at different times and in different places in Greece. Gold described by Homer as weighing a talent appears to have been a very small amount. As finally fixed by Solon, the silver talent weighed fifty-six pounds, fourteen ounces. One-sixtieth of a talent was called a *mnâ,* so that the *mnâ* in Solon's system corresponds roughly to the pound. Another weight inherited from the Greeks is the apothecary's dram (*drachmé*), one-eighth of an ounce. In modern coinage the Greek drachma, the Italian lira, and the French franc have, in normal times, retained approximately the silver value of the ancient drachma. ' Talent,' originally meaning a balance, has come to have other useful connotations through our Lord's parable.

Something of the suspicion felt toward banks by the European peasant today lurked in the heart of a Greek. There were banks, to be sure, which received deposits and paid interest on them. They were, however, mostly owned and managed by aliens rather than citizens, who rarely, and never openly, conducted such a business. The earliest mention of a Jewish banker occurs in a papyrus of the year 41 A.D. [14] But most persons preferred to hide their savings in a water jar and bury it in the field, fortunately for archaeology and the science of numismatics; or else, if they were going on a journey, to entrust the money to the care of a friend or a priest at some temple. The idea that money should be invested for the production of new wealth was grasped by only a few minds.

As institutions for lending money, the banks rendered a service which has hardly been appreciated by modern economists. Some of them have even asserted that only 'spendthrift' loans were known in antiquity, being misled by the references to such transactions in Roman comedies depicting Greek life. There, as also in Plato, it is true, one reads of a young heir falling into the clutches of an usurious money-lender, and doubtless such cases of youthful extravagance leading to extortion occurred as often as they do today. But it is not to be forgotten that the carrying trade, in which Athens was the centre of activity from the age of Pericles to that of Demosthenes, could not have been financed without loans from the banks. The risk for all concerned was great. The ships which carried wheat from the Black Sea region, slaves from Byzantium or Smyrna, raw products from the Adriatic coast, manufactured goods from Etruria in the west and Miletus in the east, were small boats only half-decked, in constant danger from the elements and from pirates. The interest charges, therefore, on loans secured by ships and their cargoes were high, sometimes amounting to three per cent a month. These rates have their modern analogy in the high premiums exacted for marine insurance.

In making loans on bottomry, a written agreement was drawn up and signed by the owner, stipulating his route and destination, the character and value of the cargo, the estimated time of the voyage, and the rate of interest. Sometimes an agreement covered only one-half of the voyage, either the outward or the inward passage. Settlement was required within twenty days after the arrival home. Sometime an inspector accompanied the owner in the interest of the money-lender. Loans on mortgages (*hypothecae*) of real estate and other property were common.

Children and adults alike kept money in small earthenware banks. These varied in shape; sometimes they were a disc-shaped box, sometimes they took the form of a shrine or building.

Since gold and silver were much less abundant then than they are now, the prices of commodities seem to be much lower, in terms of our money. With the increase in the supply of precious metals, the growth of population, and the many wars, a considerable rise in prices is noticeable from the sixth to the fourth century. In Solon's time a sheep could be bought for a drachma. This contained about eighteen cents worth of silver; but since silver was worth nearly fifty per cent more in relation to gold than it is today, its value was nearer twenty-seven cents. At the end of the fifth century the cost of a sheep had risen to eight drachmas. Again, in Solon's time a bushel and a half of barley could be bought for a drachma; in

Demosthenes' time, during a war scare, it rose
to six drachmas, considered then very high. An
unskilled slave was sold for 150 drachmas; a
highly trained one, however, capable of serving as a superintendent over factory workers,
might be worth as much as a talent, or 6,000
drachmas. Prices were so high at the end of the
Peloponnesian War that Socrates was able to
persuade a friend who had many female dependents to set them to work making garments
for sale — a hitherto unheard of thing for a
free woman.

Money undoubtedly had greater value then
than it has now, but how much greater, whether
ten times or more, it is impossible to say.
The standard of living in Athens was high as
compared with other places in Greece, yet even
there a poor cripple was content with a state
pension of only an obol (three cents) a day.
A carpenter received five or six obols a day.
A stone cutter, working on the Erechtheum and
carving marble with a delicacy and skill that
can not be matched anywhere in the world
today, received six obols.

The fare from Peiraeus to the island of
Aegina was two obols in the fourth century;
in the twentieth it is three drachmas, or nine

times as much. For two drachmas, an entire family of five persons could travel, in ancient times, from Peiraeus to Egypt.

Port duties and customs, commissions and ' rake-offs ' were as common and onerous then as now. But against these measures, operating more or less in restraint of trade, may be offset the great improvements in harbors, docks, and ship-houses for the storing of ships during the winter. In Alexandrian times, lighthouses and signals aided the mariner. In this period, also, some *entrepreneur* introduced insurance against the loss of slaves by theft or running away.

Communication by letter was difficult and intermittent. The letter, usually written on wax tablets, later on papyrus, could reach its destination only through the kindness of some traveller who chanced to be going in that direction. There was no regular post, but in the army news could be forwarded by scouts and despatch-carriers. Letters, therefore, were matters of serious thought, written only when some special exigency required. The word ' epistle ' meant originally ' injunction ' — letters were urgent requests. The following, however, written in the second century after Christ, by a ship-master to his brother, illustrates the greater ease of communication in that time, and also the crisp, yet courteous character of such correspondence: " Irenaeus to Apollinarius his brother, hearty greetings. I pray always that you may be in health, even as I am in health myself. I wish you to know that I landed on the sixth, and finished unloading on the eighteenth, and went up to Rome on the twenty-fifth. The place welcomed us as Heaven willed. We are now daily waiting for our clearance papers, but up till today none of us in the grain trade has been released. I greet your wife, also Serenus, and all who love you. Farewell." [15]

It may seem strange that the measurement of time and the establishment of a calendar were prompted by religious rather than by business motives. But business and social life moved at a more leisurely pace than they do now, whereas the gods exacted the due observance of their festivals at regular times. The phases of the moon first suggested to the priests the method of marking time's progress, the result being a lunar year, which is incommensurable, except to a very advanced astronomy, with the solar year. The calendar had therefore been thrown into great confusion by the last quarter of the fifth century, and Aristophanes whimsically pictures the wrath of the gods at finding their feast-days and fast-days hopelessly misplaced. The months, measured by the moon, were reckoned to contain alternately twenty-nine and thirty days. But this makes a total, in twelve months, of only 354 days, or more than eleven days behind the sun. Hence in a cycle of eight years, three months or ninety days were intercalated. But even with this correction the moon year fell behind the sun year, so that in two cycles, or sixteen years, there was a discrepancy of three days. The astronomer Meton, in Aristophanes' time, devised a nineteen-year cycle with seven intercalated months, which was an improvement, since in 304 years the moon was behind the sun by only five days. In Julius Caesar's time a new system was adopted which has been in use among Greeks and Russians until recently, and indeed was not abandoned in America until the eighteenth century. All reforms in the calendar have been impeded by religious conservatism, because, as we have seen, the calendar was a religious device.

The day was measured from sunset to sunset, as among the Hebrews and our Puritan ancestors; for the latter the Sabbath began on Saturday at sundown. " The evening and the morning were the first day." We still adhere unconsciously to this practice in the observance of Christmas Eve — the beginning of Christmas — All Hallow E'en, and the like. But in civil life we follow the Egyptian and Roman custom of reckoning a day from midnight to midnight. The progress of the night was noted by the help of the stars and constellations, and in army camps the night was divided into " watches." The ease with which we can observe the exact time by the " watch " on the wrist or in the waistcoat pocket is far removed from the rough and ready method which gave a name to the timepiece. In civil life the period of daylight was divided into twelve parts; this number, like the twelve months in the year, points to the duodecimal system of counting in use among the Babylonians. In the sixth century the philosopher Anaximander introduced into Europe the first time-piece, an Eastern invention. This was a simple shaft or ' obelisk ' (the Greek word for a spit), fastened upright in a place open to the sun. The ground below it was marked off into twelve feet. It was an imperfect instrument, since the length of

the ' hour ' varied with the time of year, owing
to the different lengths of the shadow. It could,
however, mark true noon, the time when the
shadow was least, and it could indicate the time
of the solstice. The latter was important, because the civil year in Athens began with the
first new moon after the summer solstice, and
the time for the celebration of the Olympic
Games was indicated in the same way. The
time for dinner was said to be " at twelve
feet "; and the comic poet Eubulus tells of a
man who, not noticing that it was the moon,
instead of the sun, which cast the shadow
at twelve feet, ran to a dinner fearing that he
was late, and arrived at dawn. An improved
sun-dial consisted of a hollow basin or hemisphere, representing the vault of the sky, with
its axis set north and south. An index was fixed
to the axis, its shadow marking the time on
the lines which were drawn on the hemisphere.

Still later, the water-clock, analogous to the
sand-glass, came to be used in the law-courts
for measuring the time of speeches. Ten gallons
of water, in ordinary cases, were allowed to
drip through a small hole in a bronze or earthenware vessel. Here again the method was imperfect, in that the hole would contract or ex-

pand, according to the temperature, at different seasons of the year.

It goes without saying, therefore, that the different parts of the day were denoted by rather general terms. The time of sunrise, noon, and sunset were the only points that could be exactly determined and accurately expressed. Similarly, the Greek was apt to divide the year somewhat vaguely into two seasons, winter and summer. Summer, for him, began with the heliacal rising of the Pleiades, in early May. Spring announced itself by the rise of the west wind, ' zephyr,' by the rising of Arcturus, and by migrating birds; in the latter case, to be sure, he would say that " one swallow does not make a spring." Winter began with the heliacal setting of the Pleiades, in November. At that time the skipper put up his boat for the winter, and waited for the calmer waters of late February, when the halycon was said even to build its nest on the smooth surface of the ocean.

2. SLAVES

ALTHOUGH, as it has already been shown, the industry of the free artisan, the free farmer, and the free tradesman abounded in Greece, especially on the mainland, yet at no time did

the ancient world rid itself of the institution
of slavery. It was assumed, even in the minds
of belated defenders of it like Aristotle, that
the inferiority of some men destined them
naturally to the enforced service of those more
advanced. Therein Aristotle showed a duller
vision of the facts and of the future than Plato,
who at least condemns the enslavement of
Greeks by Greeks, a practice generally recognized as right in war. But if any Greek, even
Plato himself, might be sold into captivity by
marauding soldiers or pirates, it becomes obvious that the assumption of natural inferiority
breaks down, and by the fourth century, before Aristotle, many voices were raised in protest against " the divine institution." Euripides,
denounced on other grounds as a freethinker
by Aristophanes, paved the way for the changing sentiment by his openly expressed sympathy for the slave and his lot.

And yet the treatment of slaves in Athens
was on the whole humane, especially if they
were house slaves, and not members of large
gangs working in remote places like the silver
mines at Laurium. Compassion marked the
character of the Athenians above all peoples
in antiquity. " No Athenian," says an orator

of the fourth century, " would willingly kill a slave," and Plato, in the *Euthyphro,* describes the keen conscience of a young man who felt it his duty to bring legal proceedings against his father because the father had by his neglect caused the death of one of his slaves. One has only to contrast the Romans and the Spartans in this regard to be convinced of the higher standards of humanity which the Athenians cherished. Athenian masters were regarded as lax by the Spartans, probably because their own treatment of the Helots, or serfs, was notoriously cruel, and in keeping with Spartan austerity. Even in Attica, however, slaves were apt to run away, especially in wartime, when on one occasion, two thousand went over to the enemy. But no insurrection of slaves in Attica occurred before the Roman domination, and the fact that they were called " children " by their masters indicates the kindly relation maintained between master and servant.

Their number has been much exaggerated. Assuming that the citizen population of Attica, about 435 B.C., amounted to about 150,000, it is probable that 100,000 slaves, at the most, were in the service of these families, and of the families of resident aliens. In some industries, a factory might employ over a hundred, not necessarily owned by one master. Yet even in industrial cities like Athens, Miletus, and Corinth, there were more free laborers than slaves; and when Athens, in the Hellenistic Age, came to be outstripped by Alexandria as a centre of wealth and commerce, her slave population decreased still more. In households of the wealthier sort the slaves numbered from two to seven.

Slaves were usually prisoners of war or captives from inferior races in Thrace, Asia Minor, and the East; or they were the native-born children of slaves, and more rarely, children abducted from free parents. But against such kidnapping the law was severe, prescribing death for conviction.

3. LOCOMOTION

ONLY within the last hundred years have the means of getting about in the world been improved over those known to the Greeks. Fortunately for them, the sea with its numerous islands tempted them to the use of ships, and thus afforded the easiest mode of transportation. The Pacific Ocean was discovered by Balboa centuries before our continent could be traversed from coast to coast. Similarly the Greek navigator, by the eighth century B.C., had explored the Mediterranean from the Black Sea to the Pillars of Heracles, while travel in the interior was impossible, or very slow and difficult. By Aristotle's time he knew something of the coast of Spain, of France, and of Britain, but the steppes of Russia and the forests by the Danube remained forbidden territory.

The ships of commerce were at best small, lumbering craft, not over a hundred feet in length, with one or two masts square-rigged, and with two oars projecting at the stern as rudders. They had a quarter deck, sometimes also a forecastle deck, but the hold remained open. They were of light draft and without a keel, which obliged the skipper to wait for a favoring wind before he could leave port. Yet, in spite of these drawbacks, the enterprising merchant managed to transport valuable cargoes, including horses and cattle.

The man-of-war was longer and of narrow beam, and though it carried a mast and sails for long distances, in fighting it was propelled by oars.

On land the traveller proceeded on foot, or rode a mule or donkey or horse. He had no saddle or stirrups, but for women and cripples a kind of pillion was provided. The bits resembled those in use today, either straight-bar or snaffle, and the headstalls and reins were like those now used.

Most of the roads were simple mountain trails worn by men or animals moving in single file. But wherever a road led to an ancient shrine, it was apt to be a cart road, for the cart appears to have been invented for religious purposes, to ensure the stately progress of an image of the god, or the priest belonging to the shrine, or, in very early times, the king. In Greece, therefore, the cart remained a somewhat exceptional vehicle for transportation down to the fifth century. Even then it was usually a farm implement, mounted on two solid wheels without springs. Oxen or mules were yoked to the pole; oxen were driven by a goad, mules by reins and a whip. There were no traces.

The chariot, after Homer's time, was used for racing, rarely for transportation. Two horses were yoked to it, and often a third and fourth horse were hitched to the yoke-horses. In the latter case traces were used and fastened to the forward rim of the chariot. The chariot board had room for two persons. The wheels were not solid, as in the case of the cart, but had four spokes. The wheels in both cart and chariot were secured to the axle by a linch-pin.

4. THE HIGHER PROFESSIONS

WE have already noticed the professions of teacher and physician. It remains to ask who were the forerunners in Greek society of the lawyer, the clergyman, the musician, the artist, and the man of letters. The Sophists, as we saw, pointed the way to the career of a university professor, introducing a higher education to supplement the elementary training taught by the despised teacher of reading and writing.

The arts and sciences in themselves were highly esteemed by the intellectual Athenians. So long as they were pursued by a gentleman of leisure they were regarded with respect. But when they were taken up as means to a livelihood they passed over into the domain of " vulgar," as opposed to " liberal," arts. The men who practiced the latter were " free," they were not dependent on their fellow men for subsistence.

Yet, in spite of popular suspicion, the idea

of a paid profession conjoined with a respectable social position was bound to win its way, and by the fourth century there was little adverse comment against it. In that period, in which professionalism of all sorts arose, there were special teachers of military tactics, who also taught the use of spear and sword. Professional gymnasts encouraged the training of young men in athletics, *i.e.*, the art of winning prizes at the public games. Experts in music and dancing taught the choruses which were to compete in dramatic and lyric contests. The later disciples of Socrates, even Plato's nephew Speusippus, came to exact pay for instruction in philosophy and other subjects.

In the latter part of the fifth century the requirement that every party to a lawsuit must conduct his own case gave rise to a new profession, that of " speech-writer." Thus arose the modern lawyer; for, though it was later permitted to call in a friend to help one in presenting his case, the party directly concerned in the suit must still appear to begin the prosecution or the defence, as the case might be. The speech-writer, then, was the one consulted on the law involved. He studied the case and prepared a speech for his client, who committed

it to memory and recited it before the court.
Practiced orators like Lysias and Demosthenes,
who had lost their property and were forced
to earn a living, thus became speech-writers
for other men. These were men of probity,
although Demosthenes was once accused by his
enemies of serving in this way both parties to
a suit. But there were other men versed in
the law who were not so respectable. These
were ready, with facile eloquence, to bring
trumped-up charges against rich men, unless
their mouths were stopped by money. They
were blackmailers, who were known as "in-
formers," and at one time threatened to defeat
all justice in the courts. Modern life has not
found it possible to purge itself entirely of this
kind of parasite, but bar associations have developed an ethics which makes it harder for
him to exist within the profession.

From the earliest times in Greece the musician received honors and rewards in his community. For the Homeric minstrel there was
a comfortable seat in the centre of the hall and
a choice cut from the meat of sacrifice. More
substantial rewards came with the expanding
community life, and the famous Arion, a citizen of Corinth, journeyed far and wide in

[134]

Italy and Sicily on a concert tour and returned, as Herodotus says, "laden with presents." Still later these men made what seemed like royal progresses from city to city. Besides giving recitals, they accepted pupils, and the stories told of them show that the "artistic temperament" is no new thing. Timotheus, who by his playing "could swell the soul to rage, or kindle soft desire," exacted from a pupil who came to him from another master double the fee that he charged to one wholly untaught.[16]

The rhapodist made a living by reciting the Homeric poems at the great festivals, prefacing the recital by one of the so-called *Homeric hymns*. He was not himself a composer or author, but rendered a great service to literature in an age when complete copies of Homer were not numerous, as custodians of the text. He also had pupils.

The great painters sold their pictures, both mural and easel, at high prices. Zeuxis received 400 minae, or six and two-thirds talents, for decorating the palace of King Archelaus of Macedon. This, in purchasing power, fairly represents a sum commonly paid by a millionaire for an old master today. On the other hand, Zeuxis held his art so high that he gave away some of his works as beyond all mere commercial price.

The sculptors likewise earned large sums for their work. Polycleitus received a hundred talents for his bronze statue of the boy tying a band round his head — the " Diadoumenos " — copies of which, in marble, are well-known. This sum must have been exceptional, especially in the fifth century, when genius abounded in many competitors for public favor.

The poets had to depend on individual patronage, and literature never entirely freed itself from this handicap until the end of the eighteenth century. Some books, even today, can be published only by private subsidies. All the greater was the need of a patron at a time when the multiplication of manuscript books was a slow and difficult process, and when no reward in royalties and no protection by copyright were available. These are quite modern devices.

For the drama the Athenian public expended large sums, but these went to the actors or were devoted to the training of the chorus. Actors, like musicians, were noted for their care of the person, their love of dress and jewelry, their erratic and whimsical moods.

But whereas the modern actor likes to have the last speech, or "curtain," the ancient actor preferred the opening lines. The fourth century witnessed the height of their art and popular favor, but Aristotle raises the question why actors in his day were men of unsound character. He answers it by saying that they had no settled abode and no time for gentlemanly culture, and were the victims of changing favor and fortune, resulting in alternate wealth and poverty.

As for historians and philosophers, they could expect little or no pecuniary reward. Fame and the satisfaction of scientific curiosity were the only spurs that urged them on.

The experts in religion ranged from the soothsayer and interpreter of dreams, up to the priest attached to a rich temple. There was also the class known as "exegetes," who were not priests, but expounders of ritual and cult practice, analogous to the lay authorities in canon law of our time. Religious teaching with an ethical message was imparted by philosophers or quasi-philosophers like Pythagoras or Empedocles. Homer and Hesiod, as Herodotus says, were regarded as giving a certain sanction to ideas about the gods which became the consensus of opinion in the entire race. But varying legends and cult practices made it possible for a considerable freedom of individual opinion to coexist with a general conformity in worship. The Greek religion, on the whole, is a capital refutation of the eighteenth century theory that religion arose from the craft and chicanery of priests.

A marked secular character distinguished Greek religion. Only a few priests were obliged to practice celibacy, and the person of a priest was not always inviolable. Every father of a family could offer sacrifice without priestly intervention, and some priesthoods were annual offices. As in country districts of Greece today, the priest might carry on other vocations. Within the precinct of his temple, of course, his authority was absolute. He was the only sacrificant there, he granted the right of asylum to a fugitive at his altar, he kept order and was responsible for the protection of the precinct and the cult image. He wore full, flowing robes, — white, if he were a priest of the Olympian gods, purple, if he were attached to the shrine of an underworld god. His authority was symbolized in the staff which he carried wound with fillets; he usually wore long hair, on which, when performing his office, he wore a wreath of myrtle, or laurel, or olive. So the priests of the Greek church wear their hair in a long coil today (except, by special dispensation, in America), and the ease with which they pass to secular occupations is a part of the inheritance from paganism.

V. IN THE TEMPLE

WE HAVE seen that the ritual for the dead proceeded from the belief that man possesses a soul distinct from the body, — a dread mysterious something which he recognizes in dreams and trances, and which leaves the body forever at death. The soul of the dead man must be tended and placated, and since its wants and place of abode after death are uncertain, it must be supplied for its journey to the underworld with offerings and gifts which it had valued in this life. The worship of ancestors can be traced back to the middle of the second millennium before Christ in the tombs of the Mycenaean kings.

The Greek felt that in his daily life he was constantly surrounded by beings of the spirit world. Every tree and cave, every river and spring, had its divinity; wherever a house was to be built, the spirits of the place must be appeased and invoked to render protection to the new dwelling. The very tiles on the roof

were under the watchful care of a spirit or
' heros,' the portal or the hinges of the door
had their protecting ' Apollo ' or ' Hermes,' the
street corners were consecrated to Hecate or
Artemis (' Diana of the Crossroads '). Everywhere he turned, the Greek was conscious of the
' daemoniac ' presence, and while Socrates is the
first to give a spiritual and ethical conception to
its influence, who shall say that the Greek before him was moved wholly by superstitious
fears to pay this reverence? He believed in
ghosts, and strove to lay them with magic; but
he also believed in gods of pity and justice and
protection, and rendered them sacrifice and
service according to his means, and this higher
belief found expression in statues, temples,
shrines, and groves of unsurpassed beauty. It
took time, to be sure, to win to the higher
conceptions of the gods. Within a few steps of
the radiant figure of Athena of the Parthenon,
the gold and ivory statue of Pheidias' genius,
the priests of Artemis kept up an old ritual in
which little girls, of the best families in Athens,
danced before the goddess dressed as bears.
And the older animal worship was remembered
in epithets like ' Ox-eyed ' Hera, ' Owl-eyed '
Athena, Apollo, ' Defender against Wolves.'

The serpent lives on today as a symbol of medicine because Asklepios, god of healing, was regularly figured with a serpent. Art idealized, but did not entirely hide, the original meaning of Pan, who had the foot of a goat, or of the Centaurs, half horse and half man, or of the satyrs with horses' tails.

What advanced intellects like Socrates and Plato thought of these figments we know. They accepted them as a part of the great and reverent religion of their fathers, reserving to themselves the right to reject any stories about them that detracted from the dignity and the goodness of the deity. So the Greek immigrant in America learns to feel some shame at the mention of the Kalikantzari, or spirits that walk the earth at Christmas time. Yet he never quite denies their existence. All Greeks maintained a close and intimate relation with their gods, and never began even a banquet without a libation to the ' Good Spirit.' They consulted the gods, aided by soothsayers or by men versed in the laws of religion (exegetes), through dreams, oracles, omens, and the flight of birds, before undertaking any important business. Even humor, which Judaism and Christianity have banished from religion, is not

excluded from their thought of the relation of
men to the gods.[17] In all conceptions of the
nature of the god-head the Greek was fortified
by his knowledge of Homer and Hesiod acquired in school, — a knowledge which later
passed to the western world and enriched its
literature and art with the radiant figures of
Zeus and Aphrodite, fauns and nymphs, Helen
and Achilles.

And yet we must recognize, for all the authority of Homer, that the Greeks possessed
no sacred scriptures entirely comparable to
the *Bible* of Christians, the *Koran* of Moslems,
the *Talmud* of the Jews, or the *Vedas* of the
Hindus. There existed, it is true, religious
hymns overlaid with poetry; there were
exegetes to whom a worshipper in doubt might
go to find out what was ' the custom of the
fathers ' in any question of rite or duty. But
the priests never constituted an authorita-
tive hierarchy, and often, like priests of rural
parishes in the Greek Church today, they engaged in other occupations beside their priest-
hood. A theology with hard and fast dogmas
was lacking. Heresy hunting was rare, and if
it seems to occur at all, as in the popular outbursts against Anaxagoras and Socrates, it was

more often the result of a conviction inspired
by demagogues that the ' atheist ' on trial had
contravened the authority of the state.

The Greek habit of referring all the acts of
life to the protection of the gods resulted in
the founding of many institutions, like the
national sports and the theatre, which today
have become entirely secular and unrelated to
religion. The dedication of sport to the gods
was prompted by the ' agonistic' spirit, the de-
light in a competition (*agon*) which is noticeable in Greeks from the earliest times. This
spirit controlled many other activities, the
speeches in the law-courts, the contests of
dramatic poets in the theatre, the clash of wills
in tragedy itself. In sport, there were the gymnic, the hippic, and the musical competition.
In the gymnic contests, athletes competed
naked for prizes in running, the broad jump,
throwing the discus, hurling the spear, and
wrestling. These five events constituted the
pentathlon run off in the stadium. The pankration combined boxing and wrestling, and was
regarded as the severest of all contests. The
hippic contests arose later than Homer, when
horses had become a sign of wealth and the
racing of chariots for sport had displaced their

use in war. There were also races on horseback and races with mules hitched to carts;
and in spite of the humorous possibilities, even
Pindar did not disdain to write odes celebrat-
ing victorious races with mules. One spectacu-
lar variety, a relay race on horseback, wherein
the riders handed on lighted torches from one
to another, has left a fine bit of imagery in our
language today. The musical *agon* comprised
choral odes, singing to the lyre, playing the
flute (thus introducing instrumental virtuos-
ity), the recitation of epic poetry by rhap-
sodists, and later the declamations of orators,
historians, and others who wrote in the method
or with the purpose of the modern essay. The
ten tribes of Attica competed in song with
choruses of fifty men or fifty boys, all of whom
had undergone special training, with careful
attention even to diet, for a period of ten
months before the competition. Thus arose, in
a few years, a large body of citizens who loved
music and could appreciate and criticize musical performances with no uncertain voice or
standards. Greek community singing far transcended, in ambitious scope, similar efforts
today.

The *Panathenaea,* a great festival held in

summer every four years in glorification of Athena, tutelar goddess of Athens, became the centre upon which all these interests especially converged. On this occasion regattas also were held, including both sailing and rowing contests. Other arts contributed their share, and the sculptor Pheidias left an undying memorial of the whole festival in the Panathenaic frieze which he and his assistants made for the cella of the Parthenon. Men on prancing horses, the pride of the aristocratic cavalry, attendants leading animals for the sacrifice, women carrying sacrificial utensils, officials bearing olive branches, priests making ready the robe of the goddess which had been woven and embroidered by daughters of citizens proud to be chosen for this honor, and last, the serene figures of the gods themselves, are shown in panoramic completeness. The whole effect is moving in its simple perfection, in its eternally right proportion of manhood and god-head, freedom and order, rest and action.

This was the festival in which every Athenian might partake without money and without price, in his native city. It included a vast procession of worshippers from the market-place to the temple on the Acropolis. A ship mounted on wheels — surviving in the modern 'float' — bore on its mast the robe destined for the statue. But there were four other festivals, in which all Greeks might join, from whatever part of the world, also held four years apart. The most celebrated were the Olympic Games, held in Olympia, a small village of Elis. With scarcely any interruption they were kept up for the extraordinary period of twelve hundred years. In the fourth century of our era they were stopped by the Emperor Theodosius, and Olympia became more deserted and forlorn than a college playground in the summer vacation. The games were revived by the athletes of the modern world in 1896. The other Panhellenic festivals, mostly athletic, but allowing other contests also, were the Pythian in honor of the Apollo of Delphi; the Nemean, a festival to Zeus in the little town of Nemea; and the Isthmian, in Corinth, to which Saint Paul alludes with the words: "I have fought the good fight, I have finished the course."

One aspect of popular cult has left its influence where it might least be suspected, in the theatre. For the Greek drama sprang from the worship of Dionysus, god of all the life-giving and reproductive forces of nature. After the vintage, wherein the bounteous god had bestowed upon his worshippers the reward of the summer's toil in the grapes and wine which were under his protection, he seemed to withdraw, in the cold and the storms of winter. It was needful, therefore, about the time of the winter solstice, to coax the god back to his land and people. A tree, preferably an evergreen, was brought from the forest and set up near his altar. Upon it the worshippers hung ribbons and cakes, symbolical of summer fruit and plenty, in order to remind him and them of his life-giving function. Thus arose the festival, held annually in the country districts, which was called the "Rural Dionysia." Again, in the early spring, the god was invoked in the festival of Dionysus of the Wine-Vat, "the Lenaea." In both of these, hymns called "dithyrambs" were sung in his praise, recounting his triumphs and defeats among men. The worshippers masqueraded in all sorts of animal shapes, and soon the spirit of mimicry prompted one of the worshippers to assume the guise of Dionysus himself. Borne in upon a cart among the company of singers and dancers, he was acclaimed as the god, and thus

became the first actor, describing by voice and
gesture his adventures. He wore a mask, as did
all actors later, and his function as 'answerer'
or 'interpreter' gave him the name which sur
vives in 'hypocrite.' The sole essential in thi
early 'drama' or representation of 'thing
done,' was the circular dancing ground, called
'orchestra,' with the altar of the god in the
centre.

As time passed, and the rural festival was
included in the great town celebration in
Athens known as the "City Dionysia," Aeschy
lus added a second actor, and thus justified
his title as the Father of Tragedy. For only
with a second actor could the poet adequately
represent the conflict of will which is of the
essence of tragedy. Since these two actors per
formed several rôles in the course of a play
a tent or booth (*skené*) was erected near the
orchestra wherein they changed costumes and
masks. Sophocles conceived the idea of making
this *skené* a more permanent building at a tan
gent to the 'orchestra' opposite the spectators
and decorated it so as to make a fitting back
ground or 'scene' for the play. He also intro
duced a third actor. We thus have all the
essentials of a theatre, the audience seating

themselves on the hillside at the southeastern slope of the Acropolis.

As a reminder of the origins, since the new art had sprung from crude songs in honor of the god, the band of singers, called ' chorus ' because they also danced, remained the central and essential feature of a play in the great period.

In reading a Greek play today we must imagine the added effects of the music and the dancing; in the latter there was much pantomime. The high seriousness which distinguishes tragedy, especially Greek tragedy, was given to it at the beginning by the sombre genius of men like Aeschylus and Phrynichus, who lived at a time of grave turbulence and danger to the state. Comedy had even ruder beginnings, but though it was inspired by the same worship of Dionysus, it did not receive recognition in urban centres until a later time.

It was not until the latter part of the fourth century that the drama became more secular in character, and even then an old-fashioned citizen would have found it hard to regard it merely as a worldly spectacle, entirely divorced from religious sanction. Throughout the entire period of Athenian productivity in the arts it was recognized as a powerful educative force. "Little boys," says Aristophanes, "have their schoolmasters to teach them; grown-ups have the poets." By poets he meant the playwrights of his day.

Through the National Games, during which a truce from all warfare was proclaimed throughout the Greek world, the Greeks were bound together in a consciousness of racial unity as by no other force. Neither politics, nor a common speech, nor the threat of foreign invasion had even an approximate influence for union and harmony. The first approach to federalization may be seen in the union of states in a common worship, like that of Apollo in Delos and at Delphi, and in spite of lamentable failures, these "Amphictionies" — associations of "neighbors" — were able to mitigate some of the cruelties of war, were, in fact, the first dream of a Hague Court, of a Geneva Convention, of a League of Nations. In this consciousness of the bond of religion the modern descendants of the men who conceived these unions are like them. Torn by political differences, religion is still for the Greeks a powerful force for solidarity in the whole people.

NOTES AND BIBLIOGRAPHY

NOTES

1. T. Zielinski, *Die Antike und Wir*, Leipzig, 1911, page 66 ff.

2. *E.g.*, the ʿΗδυπάθεια, or *High Living*, of Archestratus, a contemporary of Aristotle. Most of the works on cookery mentioned in the ancient authors were parodies in verse of earlier text-books (τέχναι) on the subject. See Athenaeus, 4 e.

3. That the celebrated Aspasia was an *hetaera* is not borne out by the scanty evidence concerning her, Wilamowitz to the contrary notwithstanding. See Judeich in Pauly-Wissowa, *Realencyclopädie*,[2] *s.v.* " Aspasia." At any rate she became Pericles' second wife (*ca.* 445 B.C.?), and is said to have influenced him to undertake the Samian War, much as the Empress Eugénie was accused of causing the Franco-Prussian War.

4. See Gilbert Murray, *Our Great War and the Great War of the Ancient Greeks*, New York, 1920, for some interesting analogies between the most destructive war in Greek history and the European War of 1914.

5. Milton, *L'Allegro:*

> " There let Hymen oft appear
> In saffron robe, with taper clear,
> And pomp, and feast, and revelry."

Spenser, *Epithalamion:*
" And evermore they Hymen, Hymen sing,
That al the woods them answer, and theyr eccho ring."
In the sentence " the bride was led to the hymeneal altar " (James Grant) there is a mixture of pagan and Christian.

6. Galen, XVII. B. 145. The line quoted is *Iliad*, XXI. 107.

NOTES

7. For the oath in full see H. O. Taylor, *Greek Biology and Medicine,* page 34. (In the Series: *Our Debt to Greece and Rome.*)

8. G. Milligan, *Selections from the Greek Papyri,* Cambridge, England, 1910, page 5.

9. See D. E. Smith, *Mathematics,* in this Series.

10. *Anthologia Graeca,* IV. 244 (Jacobs).

11. Matthew Arnold has caught the poetry of this early adventure in commerce in these verses of *The Scholar-Gipsy:*

> " As some grave Tyrian trader, from the sea,
>   Descried at sunrise an emerging prow
> Lifting the cool-hair'd creepers stealthily,
> The fringes of a southward-facing brow
>   Among the Aegean isles;
>   And saw the merry Grecian coaster come
>   Freighted with amber grapes, and Chian wine,
>   Green bursting figs, and tunnies steep'd in brine;
>   And knew the intruders on his ancient home."

12. The well-known inscription of Abu-Simbel, dating before 589 B.C. See E. S. Roberts, *An Introduction to Greek Epigraphy,* Cambridge, England, 1887, Part 1, page 151.

13. *Cf.* J. A. K. Thomson, *Greeks and Barbarians.* This fondness for the preposterous is what is commonly known as " Yankee humor." But it is equally Greek.

14. U. Wilcken, *Archiv für Papyrusforschung,* Leipzig, 1908; IV. 567.

15. Milligan, *op. cit.,* page 100. The delay in Rome exasperated the skipper, yet the euphemism by which he indicates his vexation is to be contrasted with the language of a modern ship-captain in a similar case. " Welcomed us as Heaven willed " would be, *Anglicè* and *Americanicè,* " we had a hell of a time."

16. Quintilian, II. 3. 3. The airs and graces of a temperamental prima donna are delightfully pictured in Theocritus, *Idyl* 15.

17. *E.g.,* Zeus, enthroned in Heaven, laughs at the

pranks of his infant son Apollo, greedy to possess the
lucrative shrine at Delphi (Euripides, *Iphigenia among the
Taurians,* 1274 ff). For the kindly humor permitted by
mediaeval Christianity, compare the oxen carved in stone
on the roof of the Cathedral at Laon — intimate friends
and helpers of the builders.

BIBLIOGRAPHY

A full list of works on the subject published prior to 1902 will be found in the author's *Life of the Ancient Greeks* (D. Appleton and Co.), 1902.

ABRAHAMS, ETHEL B., *Greek Dress*. London, 1913.

BAUMGARTEN, F., POLAND, F., and WAGNER, R., *Die Hellenische Kultur.*[3] Leipzig and Berlin, 1908.

BLÜMNER, H., *Leben und Sitten der Griechen*. 3 vols. Leipzig, 1887. Translation, *The Home Life of the Ancient Greeks*, by Alice Zimmern. London, 1895.

BOTSFORD, G. W., and SIHLER, E. G., *Hellenic Civilization*, in *Records of Civilization* (J. T. Shotwell, Editor). New York, 1915.

BURNS, C. Delisle, *Greek Ideals, A Study of Social Life*. London, 1917.

CHAPOT, COLIN, CROISET, HATZFELD, JARDÉ, JOUQUET, LEROUX, REINACH, *L'Hellénisation du monde antique*. Paris, 1914.

DAREMBERG, C., et SAGLIO, E., *Dictionnaire des antiquités grecques et romaines d'après les textes et les monuments*. Paris, 1873–1919.

DAVIS, W. S., *A Day in Old Athens*. Boston (n.d.).
A Victor of Salamis. New York and London, 1907.

DICKINSON, G. LOWES, *The Greek View of Life.*[12] London, 1919.

FOUGÈRES, G., *La vie publique et privée des Grecs et des Romains*. Paris, 1894.

GAINES, C. K., *Gorgo, A Romance of Old Athens*. Boston, 1903.

GARDINER, E. NORMAN, *Greek Athletic Sports and Festivals*. London, 1910.

GARDNER, E. A., *Ancient Athens*. New York, 1907.

BIBLIOGRAPHY

GARDNER, P., and JEVONS, F. B., *A Manual of Greek Antiquities*. London and New York, 1895.

GREENE, W. C., *The Achievement of Greece*. Cambridge, Massachusetts, 1923.

LAWSON, J. C., *Modern Greek Folklore and Ancient Greek Religion*. Cambridge, England, 1910.

MAHAFFY, J. P., *Social Life in Greece, from Homer to Menander*. London, 1894–1913.

What Have the Greeks Done for Civilization? New York and London, 1909.

McCLEES, HELEN, *The Daily Life of the Greeks and Romans*. (illustrated) New York (Metropolitan Museum), 1924.

POLAND, F., REISINGER, E., and WAGNER, R., *Die antike Kultur*. Leipzig and Berlin, 1922.

RANSOM, CAROLINE L., *Studies in Ancient Furniture: Couches and Beds of the Greeks, Etruscans, and Romans*. Chicago, 1905.

RIDER, BERTHA C., *The Greek House*. Cambridge, England, 1916.

SCHREIBER, T., *Atlas of Classical Antiquities*, edited by W. C. F. Anderson. London, 1895.

SMITH, SIR WM., WAYTE, W., and MARINDIN, G. E., *A Dictionary of Greek and Roman Antiquities*.[3] 2 volumes. London, 1914.

SNEDEKER, CAROLINE D., *The Spartan. New York*, 1911.

The Perilous Seat. New York, 1923.

THOMSON, J. A. K., *The Greek Tradition*. London and New York, 1915.

Greeks and Barbarians. London and New York, 1921.

TUCKER, T. G., *Life in Ancient Athens*. New York and London, 1906.

VAN HOOK, LARUE, *Greek Life and Thought*. New York, 1923. (See Bibliography.)

WHIBLEY, L. (Editor), *A Companion to Greek Studies*.[3] Cambridge, England, 1916.

British Museum Guide to the Exhibition illustrating Greek and Roman Life.[2] London, 1920 (illustrated).

Our Debt to Greece and Rome

AUTHORS AND TITLES

AUTHORS AND TITLES

AUTHORS AND TITLES

Aeschylus and Sophocles. *J. T. Sheppard.*

Greek Religion. *Walter Woodburn Hyde.*

Survivals of Roman Religion. *Gordon J. Laing.*

Mythology. *Jane Ellen Harrison.*

Ancient Beliefs in The Immortality of The Soul. *Clifford H. Moore.*

Stage Antiquities. *James Turney Allen.*

Plautus and Terence. *Gilbert Norwood.*

Roman Politics. *Frank Frost Abbott.*

Psychology, Ancient and Modern. *G. S. Brett.*

Ancient and Modern Rome. *Rodolfo Lanciani.*

Warfare by Land and Sea. *Eugene S. McCartney.*

The Greek Fathers. *James Marshall Campbell.*

Greek Biology and Medicine. *Henry Osborn Taylor.*

Mathematics. *David Eugene Smith.*

Love of Nature among the Greeks and Romans. *H. R. Fairclough.*

Ancient Writing and its Influence. *B. L. Ullman.*

Greek Art. *Arthur Fairbanks.*

Architecture. *Alfred M. Brooks.*

Engineering. *Alexander P. Gest.*

Modern Traits in Old Greek Life. *Charles Burton Gulick.*

Roman Private Life. *Walton Brooks McDaniel.*

Greek and Roman Folklore. *William Reginald Halliday.*

Ancient Education. *J. F. Dobson.*